WHAT EVERY PRINCIPAL SHOULD KNOW ABOUT

ETHICAL AND
SPIRITUAL
LEADERSHIP

WHAT EVERY PRINCIPAL SHOULD KNOW ABOUT LEADERSHIP
The 7-Book Collection

By Jeffrey Glanz

What Every Principal Should Know About Instructional Leadership

What Every Principal Should Know About Cultural Leadership

What Every Principal Should Know About Ethical and Spiritual Leadership

What Every Principal Should Know About School-Community Leadership

What Every Principal Should Know About Collaborative Leadership

What Every Principal Should Know About Operational Leadership

What Every Principal Should Know About Strategic Leadership

WHAT EVERY PRINCIPAL SHOULD KNOW ABOUT

ETHICAL AND SPIRITUAL LEADERSHIP

JEFFREY GLANZ

CORWIN PRESS
A SAGE Publications Company
Thousand Oaks, California

For information:

Corwin Press
A Sage Publications Company
2455 Teller Road
Thousand Oaks, California 91320
E-mail: order@corwinpress.com

Sage Publications Ltd.
1 Oliver's Yard
55 City Road
London EC1Y 1SP
United Kingdom

Sage Publications India Pvt. Ltd.
B-42, Panchsheel Enclave
Post Box 4109
New Delhi 110 017   India

Printed in the United States of America.

Library of Congress Cataloging-in-Publication Data

Glanz, Jeffrey.
What every principal should know about ethical and spiritual
leadership / Jeffrey Glanz.
    p. cm.
Includes bibliographical references and index.
ISBN 1-4129-1588-0 (pbk.)
    1. Educational leadership. 2. School principals—Conduct of life. I. Title
LB2806.4.G5323 2006
371.2'012—dc22   2005005356

This book is printed on acid-free paper.

05   06   07   08   09   10   9   8   7   6   5   4   3   2   1

Acquisitions Editor:	Elizabeth Brenkus
Editorial Assistant:	Candice L. Ling
Project Editor:	Tracy Alpern
Copy Editor:	Rachel Hile Bassett
Proofreader:	Christine Dahlin
Typesetter:	C&M Digitals (P) Ltd.
Indexer:	Gloria Tierney
Cover Designer:	Rose Storey
Graphic Designer:	Scott Van Atta

Contents

*To my mom and dad, who were the first who taught
me the obligation to behave ethically, to strive for moral
grounding, and to appreciate the enduring nature of spirit.*

Acknowledgments

Spencer Maxcy once concisely and accurately posited that "the core value of good leadership and good schools is heart." For Maxcy, remaining passionate about one's work, steadfast about one's sense of right and wrong, and committed to social justice are moral and ethical imperatives for educational leaders. Ethical principals realize fully that honest, informed, and sincere human relationships give meaning and integrity to their lives. They live within themselves. They are true to their own spirit. They are accountable to something larger than themselves. Ethical leaders understand that their work is as spiritual as it is intellectual and moral. Principals I have been privileged to know and see in action are happy and fulfilled because they view their work as spiritual, engaged, and ethical. For them, leading is about sharing, guiding, assisting, communicating, praising, encouraging . . . touching another's soul. As ethical, moral, and spiritual leaders, principals are role models for all others privileged to work for children. This book and series are dedicated to all who aspire to the principalship, currently serve as principals, or have been principals. No nobler enterprise and profession exists, for educators are the ones who foremost model a sense of ethics and spirit as they go about their work.

* * * * * * * * * * * * * * * *

Thanks to my acquisitions editor, Lizzie Brenkus, for her gentle encouragement and support. I appreciated her thoughtful highlights of reviewer comments, which helped me focus my efforts during the revision process. Never dogmatic, but always keeping the book's focus in mind, Lizzie was a pleasure to work with. Many thanks also go to Robb Clouse, editorial director, who prompted me to consider a trilogy of sorts: a book about teaching, which eventuated into *Teaching 101*; a book about assistant principals, which led to *The Assistant Principal's Handbook*; and a book about principals, which resulted to my surprise in this groundbreaking series, *What Every Principal Should Know About Leadership.*

Special thanks to my wife, Lisa, without whose support such a venture would be impossible. I love you . . . at least as much as I love writing.

Corwin Press gratefully acknowledges the contributions of the following individuals:

Albert Armer, Principal
Wortham Elementary School
Wortham, TX

Judy Carr, Associate Professor
College of Education
University of South Florida
Sarasota, FL

Robin Dexter, Assistant
    Professor
College of Education
University of Wyoming
Laramie, WY

Phil Silsby, Principal
    (retired)
Belleville West High School
Belleville, IL

Paul Young, Principal,
    Author
West Elementary School
Lancaster, OH

About the Author

 **Jeffrey Glanz**, **EdD**, currently serves as Dean of Graduate Programs and Chair of the Department of Education at Wagner College in Staten Island, New York. He also coordinates the educational leadership program that leads to New York State certification as a principal or assistant principal. Prior to arriving at Wagner, he served as executive assistant to the president of Kean University in Union, New Jersey. Dr. Glanz held faculty status as a tenured professor in the Department of Instruction and Educational Leadership at Kean University's College of Education. He was named Graduate Teacher of the Year in 1999 by the Student Graduate Association and was also that year's recipient of the Presidential Award for Outstanding Scholarship. He served as an administrator and teacher in the New York City public schools for 20 years. Dr. Glanz has authored, coauthored, or coedited 13 books and has more than 35 peer-reviewed article publications. With Corwin Press he coauthored the bestselling *Supervision That Improves Teaching* (2nd ed.) and *Supervision in Practice: Three Steps to Improve Teaching and Learning* and authored *The Assistant Principal's Handbook* and *Teaching 101: Classroom Strategies for the Beginning Teacher.* More recently he coauthored *Building Effective Learning Communities: Strategies for Leadership, Learning, & Collaboration.* Most recently, Dr. Glanz has authored the *What Every Principal Should Know About Leadership: The 7-Book Collection:*

> *What Every Principal Should Know About Instructional Leadership*
>
> *What Every Principal Should Know About Cultural Leadership*

What Every Principal Should Know About Ethical and Spiritual Leadership

What Every Principal Should Know About School-Community Leadership

What Every Principal Should Know About Collaborative Leadership

What Every Principal Should Know About Operational Leadership

What Every Principal Should Know About Strategic Leadership.

Consult his Web site for additional information: http://www .wagner.edu/faculty/users/jglanz/web/

* * * * * * * * * * * * * * *

The "About the Author" information you've just glanced at (excuse the pun . . . my name? . . . Glanz, "glance"?!) is standard author bio info you find in most books. As you'll discover if you glance at . . . I mean *read* . . . the Introduction, I want this book to be user-friendly in several ways. One of the ways is that I want to write as I would converse with you in person. Therefore, I prefer in most places to use the first person, so please excuse the informality. Although we've likely never met, we really do know each other if you think about it. We share a common passion about leadership, school building leadership to be more precise. We share many similar experiences. In an experiential, almost spiritual, sense, we have much in common. What I write about directly relates, I hope, to your lived experience. The information in this volume, as with the entire series, is meant to resonate, stir, provoke, and provide ideas about principal leadership, which is vital in order to promote excellence and achievement for all.

This traditional section of a book is titled "About the Author." The first paragraph in this section tells you what I "do," not "about" me or who I am. I won't bore you with all details "about me," but I'd like just to share one bit of info that communicates more meaningfully about "me" than the information in the first paragraph. I am (I presume like you) passionate about what I do. I love to teach, guide, mentor, learn, supervise, and lead. For me, leadership is self-preservation. Personally and professionally, I strive to do my very best, to use whatever God-given leadership talents I possess to make a difference in the lives of others. I continually strive to improve myself intellectually and socially, but also physically and spiritually. Family and community are very important to me. Building and sustaining community is integral to my professional practice. I see myself as part of a larger community of learners as we share, experience, overcome difficulties, learn from our mistakes, and in the end help others (students, colleagues, and community members) achieve their educational goals.

If any of the information in this book series touches you in any way, please feel free to contact me by using my personal e-mail address: tora.dojo@verizon.net. I encourage you to share your reactions, comments, and suggestions, or simply to relate an anecdote or two, humorous or otherwise, that may serve as "information from the field" for future editions of this work, ultimately to help others. Your input is much appreciated.

Questionnaire: Before We Get Started . . .

Directions: Using the Likert scale below, circle the answer that best represents your on-the-spot belief about each statement. The questionnaire serves as an advanced organizer of sorts for some of the key topics in this book, although items are purposely constructed in no particular order. Discussion of each topic, though, occurs within the context of relevant chapters. Responses or views to each statement are presented in a subsection following the questionnaire (this section begins "Now, let's analyze your responses . . ."). You may or may not agree with the points made, but I hope you will be encouraged to reflect on your own views. Reflective activities follow to allow for deeper analysis. Elaboration of ideas emanating from this brief activity will occur throughout the text and series. I encourage you to share reflections (yours and mine) with colleagues. I'd appreciate your personal feedback via the e-mail address I've listed in the "About the Author" section.

> SA = Strongly Agree ("For the most part, yes.")
> A = Agree ("Yes, but . . .")
> D = Disagree ("No, but . . .")
> SD = Strongly Disagree ("For the most part, no.")

SA   A   D   SD   1. Principals must have an unwavering commitment to ethical standards and conduct.

SA   A   D   SD   2. Ethical standards of performance are subjective in nature; that is, such

xiv   Ethical and Spiritual Leadership

standards depend on the point of
view of the particular principal.

SA   A   D   SD   3. Ethical standards of performance
                        should be assessed solely in terms of
                        prescribed standards from district,
                        state, or association policies.

SA   A   D   SD   4. *Ethics* and *morals* are equivalent terms.

SA   A   D   SD   5. Principals not only must promote
                        academic excellence in terms of higher
                        achievement levels as measured by
                        standardized test scores, but also must
                        work for higher-quality performances on
                        a variety of outcomes.

SA   A   D   SD   6. I am attuned to my spiritual nature.

SA   A   D   SD   7. *Spirit* is too nebulous a term to have
                        much practical use in the work of a
                        principal.

SA   A   D   SD   8. A principal who is ethical by following
                        personal and organizational moral
                        norms is also likely to think and feel
                        spiritually.

SA   A   D   SD   9. I concur with theorists such as Jean
                        Piaget that morals emerge and develop
                        as a result of interacting in a social
                        environment and that genetics play
                        an insignificant factor.

SA   A   D   SD   10. I concur with some theorists such as
                        Jean Piaget that morals are best refined
                        as the individual attempts to resolve
                        personal and social dilemmas in
                        real-life settings.

SA   A   D   SD   11. Societal and cultural beliefs greatly
                        influence one's personal sense of ethics.

SA A D SD 12. I concur with some theorists such as Lawrence Kohlberg that there is no single best way to resolve an ethical dilemma; there are no right answers.

SA A D SD 13. Principals have a moral obligation to be fair, nonjudgmental, and honest in all school and nonschool activities.

SA A D SD 14. Concepts of justice, caring, and democracy are a vital part of the work of a principal, even more so than academic performance.

SA A D SD 15. I am more spiritual than most other principals.

SA A D SD 16. I am more ethical than most other principals.

SA A D SD 17. I believe that principals must demonstrate certain character virtues, such as humility and courage.

SA A D SD 18. Universal moral imperatives of leadership, such as a commitment to democracy and an ethic of caring, are not only possible but necessary.

SA A D SD 19. Resolving moral dilemmas is easier over time and with experience.

SA A D SD 20. Although commonplace, ethical and moral dilemmas are challenging and require deep reflection about one's values and beliefs.

Before we analyze your responses, consider the fact that ethical and spiritual leadership is not always addressed in principal preparation programs to any significant degree. A concern for one's ethical conduct and remaining sensitive to one's spirit (this term will be defined later, but for now I want to purposely encourage you to explore your own meaning, because no single definition anyway suffices) is fundamentally important in order to lead with integrity and deep understanding. An ethical and spiritual leader is concerned with the following areas of leadership, among others:

- Examining one's personal and innermost beliefs and values to ensure that one acts with compassion and affirms justice for all people
- Realizing the impact of one's actions on others within the school organization
- Aligning one's personal, cultural, and even religious values with organizational codes of ethics
- Making well-reasoned decisions to moral dilemmas that do not have easy solutions
- Leading others by example
- Knowing oneself very well; one's strengths and limitations
- Remaining sensitive to circumstances or events that others may overlook
- Attuning oneself to personal convictions and organizational norms
- Knowing and sensing what others may not
- Striving for high ideals

Effective leaders build integrity and character through their work. To paraphrase Peter Drucker (1999), good leaders lead not through knowledge and skills, but through responsibility and integrity. Ethical and moral leadership is an imperative in building and sustaining effective learning communities (Sergiovanni, 1992; Starratt, 2003). Without an ethical and moral stance, a leader will lead perfunctorily, without "soul" (Bolman & Deal, 1995).

Ethics deals with actions that are commonly seen as right or wrong. Showing favoritism in hiring a colleague who is white over someone who is black is prejudicial and discriminatory; it's simply wrongheaded. An ethical leader strives to do the right things as well as to do things right. Morality deals with a system of values that undergirds ethical behavior. A moral leader might value social justice and equity for all people. If one's behavior is consistent, then one will act "morally" when the particular value is necessary in a given situation. Because a leader values social justice, she or he will consciously remain on guard for possible prejudicial behavior in selecting a new hire.

Ethical and moral dilemmas are very commonplace. The situation is not always clear. Also unclear are the standards we use to determine whether an action is ethical or unethical. How you as a leader draw upon your proclivities and sensitivities toward ethical and moral behavior will determine the extent to which you are effective in building and sustaining a learning community. How do we understand spirituality?

Remaining sensitive to who we are and to what we believe and care about talks to the spirit. Although we'll try later to clarify these terms, which are variously defined by many people, for now, it's important to remain attentive to our personal tendencies. What is it about our nature or personality that compels us to behave ethically or less so? Although not true in all cases, some people who are naturally aggressive and goal oriented may not care that their actions may hurt others as long as their needs are satisfied or goals accomplished. On the other hand, people who are not as goal driven and compulsive may not resort to unethical, immoral behavior to achieve an end. We all still must remain vigilant and conscious of who we are, what we want to accomplish, and how we intend to achieve our goals. Developing and acting on a strong system of values that nurture ethical and moral conduct is essential to remaining spiritually sensitive.

These ideas are fundamental. Consider the following questions as you consider the meaning of ethical and spiritual leadership:

Reflective Questions

1. Which of the belief statements and ideas above resonate the most with you?

2. Which of the views expressed above do you disagree with? Explain.

3. What does ethical leadership mean to you, and why is it so important, if it is? Explain.

4. What does spiritual leadership mean to you, and why is it so important, if it is? Explain.

* * * * * * * * * * * * * * * *

Examine these quotations on ethics, morality, and spirituality. What do they mean to you?

> "Just as physical life cannot exist without the support of the physical environment, so moral life cannot go on without support of a moral environment."

—John Dewey

> "Leadership is all about values. Ethics as it relates to leadership is more focused upon the determination of the good toward which the group is working and the selection of proper means for the achievement of that end."

—Spencer J. Maxcy

> "'Do we have the will to educate all children?' . . . we continue to struggle to answer it. The question invokes a sense of moral purpose or responsibility. The question carries with it a veiled accusation—that we do not have the will to do so."

—Randall B. Lindsey, Laraine M. Roberts, and Franklin CampbellJones

"According to Stephen Covey, principle-centered leaders operate in alignment with 'self-evident, self-validating natural laws.' These include such basic principles as fairness, equity, justice, honesty, trust, integrity, and service. These principles point the way for leaders."

—Joyce Kaser, Susan Mundry,
Katherine E. Stiles, and Susan Loucks-Horsley

"Principals must be ethical and aboveboard in every aspect of their lives. All decisions must be based on good judgment and basic moral and ethical standards. . . . This sounds obvious. But some ethical decisions are not so simple."

—Elaine L. Wilmore

"The wise leader models spiritual behavior and lives in harmony with spiritual values."

—John Heider

"Every organization needs to evolve for itself a sense of its own ethical and spiritual core."

—Lee G. Bolman and Terrence E. Deal

* * * * * * * * * * * * * * * *

Now, let's analyze your responses to the questionnaire:

1. Principals must have an unwavering commitment to ethical standards and conduct.
    Many believe that such an "unwavering commitment" is more important than almost anything else. You can easily gain knowledge of curriculum theory or clinical supervision, but adhering to a code of

ethics is not as easily developed. You can espouse an ethical stance, but do your actions belie your stated beliefs? Many believe that we all come into the principalship with core values gleaned from our experiences at home, church, or other social settings. If these experiences were fraught with uncertainties or insecurities, for example, then your ability to maintain an ideal ethical stance may be compromised. Principal training programs may "teach" ethics by exposing principal candidates to theoretical issues and moral dilemmas via the use of case studies. These programs, however, cannot teach you to behave ethically. Research demonstrates that professional codes of ethics do not ensure that principals will consistently make good ethical decisions (Fenstermaker, 1994). At best, you may become aware of your tendencies and attempt to control them for the positive. To a large extent, in my view, a commitment to ethical standards of behavior and conduct is very much part of one's natural constitution (Glanz, 2002). We therefore need to attract principal candidates who possess such ethical proclivities (see Chapter 3). Parenthetically, this doesn't mean to suggest that principals must possess flawless ethical virtues; we are all human beings, and we do make misjudgments.

2. Ethical standards of performance are subjective in nature; that is, such standards depend on the point of view of the particular principal.

Many individuals don't particularly believe that ethics or morality is relative (Rachels, 1986). Particular values, though, are universally accepted, at least in the place we call school. Certain values must be adhered to by a principal. Cheating on a standardized test, for instance, cannot be tolerated in one school while accepted at another. This point is obvious. Less obvious are instances when personal ethics or beliefs come into conflict with organizational expectations or mores. Balancing one's personal code of ethics with the school's is not easy at times.

3. Ethical standards of performance should be assessed solely in terms of prescribed standards from district, state, or association policies.

Codes of conduct are often prescribed by various educational associations. For instance, one particular principal association may have a stated code of ethics that includes, for instance, that a principal should act professionally by not using his or her position to further personal self-interests, or that one should not willingly make false or malicious statements about a colleague. Although similar codes may serve to establish an accepted standard for professional behavior, they have marginal value at best, in my view, to assist you in a moral crisis or dilemma. Situations are complex and do not benefit from easy answers. You cannot simply refer to a set of prescribed rules for behavior and expect a resolution. That is why it is essential for you to develop the critical awareness and thinking skills to make reasoned decisions in difficult situations or dilemmas, a topic we will discuss in more detail later in this volume.

4. *Ethics* and *morals* are equivalent terms.

For the purposes of our discussion throughout this book, the two terms may be considered synonymous.

5. Principals not only must promote academic excellence in terms of higher achievement levels as measured by standardized test scores, but also must work for higher-quality performances on a variety of outcomes.

Although as principals we are compelled to stress academic achievement above all else because of national currents aimed at greater accountability via high-stakes testing, a good principal, in my view, realizes that attention must be paid to other essential learning outcomes. I am reminded of something a prominent educator once posited, and I paraphrase: "Our job is to help children do well in life, not just in school." Encouraging students to demonstrate and act upon humane values, a sense of camaraderie, and respect for others should be one of our primary goals.

6. I am attuned to my spiritual nature.

We've alluded several times to one's spirit or spiritual side. What do we mean by the term? Many people frame the term spiritual *in nonreligious ways. Although religious, observant individuals might state that they strive for spirituality, it doesn't necessarily follow that someone must adhere to some religious doctrine in order to achieve or experience a degree of spirituality, at least in the secular sense. In the words of Ramon Gallegos Nava (2001), "Spirituality is not a set of beliefs, rituals, dogmas, symbolic meaning, or church affiliation. . . . Spirituality is an individual, natural, direct experience of that which is sacred, of that which is transcending, of the ultimate foundation, which is the essence of all that exists" (p. 128).*

Spirituality is used in this book to connote several ideas that are interrelated. Following the lead of Bolman and Deal (1997), I define spirit *or* soul *as a bedrock sense of what we believe in, what we care about, and who we really are as individuals and as principals. Bolman and Deal explain further, "Organizational ethics must ultimately be rooted in soul—an organization's understanding of its deeply held identity, beliefs, and values" (p. 352). A leader with "spirit" or "soul" possesses a well-defined value system and a deep sense of self (Hoyle, 2002). David A. Sousa (2003) also makes the point:*

> In practice, ethical and spiritual leaders make decisions and take actions that respond to, clarify, and preserve the core values of the school community. At the same time, these leaders must move themselves, their teachers, and students to recognize the importance of ethical sensitivity, judgment, and action in order to maintain a high moral and spiritual ethos within the school. (p. 186)

Soulful or spiritual leaders are also aware of their unique qualities that make them particularly effective as leaders. Conversely, they are acutely cognizant of their limitations (see Chapter 3 for a fuller discussion). Moreover, a sense of the spiritual implies that you possess an inner calm, as Barbara L. Brock and Marilyn L. Grady (2004) explain: "Spiritually healthy people have a sense of inner calm and peace. They give of themselves, but also replenish themselves spiritually by spending time alone each day. Solitude rests the spirit, refreshes the soul, and reenergizes creativity" (p. 108). As a spiritual leader, your concern transcends personal growth, as Susan Komives, Nance Lucas, and Timothy McMahon (1998) explain: "The human spirit is the core of your being that gives life its meaning. . . . Although renewing your own spirit is important, helping members of your organization renew their spirit is essential if you are to be a successful leader" (p. 293).

7. *Spirit* is too nebulous a term to have much practical use in the work of a principal.

Despite the information provided above, some of you may still feel a bit uncomfortable discussing the spiritual side of your work. If you think of spirit, though, in its simplest way, as being finely attuned to your sense of values and ethics, then perhaps the term may find relevance. Spiritual leaders are cultural leaders in that they possess a well-conceived set of beliefs and values that guide every action they take (see my volume titled What Every Principal Should Know About Cultural Leadership). *Generally, though, people who really think deeply about their craft, try to think creatively, and seek to uncover what others may not be aware of are involved in spiritual work. Principaling, if you will, is much more than a cerebral activity; it's a spirited engagement of a community of learners trying to craft and shape a vision of possibilities for students. All of us are spiritual beings, whether we acknowledge it or not. Some of us are just more in touch with our spiritual nature than others.*

8. A principal who is ethical by following personal and organizational moral norms is also likely to think and feel spiritually.

Do you believe there is a relationship between ethical and spiritual behaviors? Those who adhere to a belief system or code of ethics and who, of course, act consistently based on these values are in touch with their spiritual nature.

9. I concur with theorists such as Jean Piaget that morals emerge and develop as a result of interacting in a social environment and that genetics play an insignificant factor.

Examining the work of Kohlberg (1971) and Gilligan (1993) confirms this statement.

10. I concur with some theorists such as Jean Piaget that morals are best refined as the individual attempts to resolve personal and social dilemmas in real-life settings.

Moral thinking and behavior are developed as we attempt to resolve ethical dilemmas in schools. Written codes and prescribed rules of conduct can only set parameters or expectations. Moral and ethical thinking are clarified as we attempt to solve real problems in real settings through critical thinking and moral decision making. According to Strike and Soltis (1998), "Ethical decision making is not just following the rules or applying the right moral principle and sticking to it no matter what" (p. 121). They assert that it is only when we apply our ideas to a real situation that we can refine our moral decision-making abilities.

11. Societal and cultural beliefs greatly influence one's personal sense of ethics.

Hopkins (1997) concurs, stating, "Research studies . . . clearly indicate that both individual and organizational ethics are influenced by cultural value systems . . . that the value system of a given culture determines the nature of the ethical paradigm subscribed to by groups and individuals residing in that culture" (p. 53).

12. I concur with some theorists, such as Lawrence Kohlberg, that there is no single best way to resolve an ethical dilemma; there are no right answers.

Wrong answers, yes; correct answers, no. Many don't believe in moral relativism, that is, that all ideas or actions are correct because they must be viewed within the cultural or personal context in which they occur. The relativistic idea of "to each his own" is simplistic and belies the complexities involved in making decisions about moral dilemmas we confront. Many concur with Strike and Soltis (1998), who explain, "The world is not neat and simple. Objective and rational discussion in moral matters offers no guarantee of successful reflective equilibrium in every case, but it does offer more promise for moral growth and moral sensitivity than does a relativistic policy of 'to each his own'" (p. 121).

13. Principals have a moral obligation to be fair, nonjudgmental, and honest in all school and nonschool activities.

Most definitely. Still, an important idea to consider is that although two individuals may agree to be "fair," their interpretations of "fairness" may vary greatly. Sam reports, "Well, I was fair-minded; I did consider all perspectives." Whereas Juan might retort, "Well, you didn't ask me!?!" Therefore, although two principals may espouse a belief in fairness, each may act upon the belief in a subjective manner assuming that he or she has indeed acted fairly; this fact of human nature complicates ethical decision making. Moreover, two individuals who share a common belief may act differently because their reasoning process differs. For example, Bill and Carlos, as high school principals, are both committed to hiring competent female math teachers. For simplicity's sake, let's say each principal interviews two competent individuals, one male and one female. Bill interviews a male teacher candidate, Steve, after interviewing many others who were less competent. In Bill's mind, he needs a teacher soon, so he intends to make the offer the next day. In the meantime, two other candidates file for the position that same day; Bill interviews them both and finds that the female candidate, Jane, is very qualified, as qualified as Steve. The same scenario occurs to Carlos. In the end, Bill hires Steve, whereas Carlos hires Jane.

Both are committed to the ethic of fairness, but each rationalizes differently. Bill feels morally obligated to Steve, because Steve was the first candidate of choice, but Carlos selects Jane, an equally qualified candidate, because the math department has no female teachers. Each will argue that he acted fairly, even justly. Hopkins (1997) makes the point that "although individuals from different backgrounds can have the same moral values they may behave differently when faced with a common situation because of the reasoning process through which they apply codes of ethics" (p. 61).

14. Concepts of justice, caring, and democracy are a vital part of the work of a principal, even more so than academic performance.
Most definitely; see Conclusion for a brief discussion of what I consider the moral imperatives of principal leadership.

15. I am more spiritual than most other principals.

16. I am more ethical than most other principals.
Obviously, your assessment of your own sense of spirit and ethics is personal. What evidence, though, can you cite to support your contention? Can or would others verify your self-assessment? All of us need to reflect deeply about our spiritual and ethical states. Through such reflection, I'm certain we'll consider shortfalls in each area; after all, no one is perfect. Personally, although I consider myself spiritual and ethical, I know I have not always lived up to those standards I value. Sometimes, for instance, I'm so busy and compulsively driven that I forget to step back for a period of reflection or deep thought. As one of my colleagues once advised, "Jeffrey, step back and smell the roses once in a while." I've also acted unethically. Although I can rationalize my actions based on personal insecurities or lapses in judgment, I know I am hard on myself and work diligently to do better next time. Each of us who is naturally inclined toward the spiritual and ethical can improve with experience, critical thought, and reflective practice.

17. I believe that principals must demonstrate certain character virtues, such as humility and courage.
This book is not morally neutral. I do believe that principals are obligated, given the nature of their role and position, to personify certain virtues, as I'll outline in more detail in Chapter 3. These virtues represent, to my mind, moral imperatives for working in the principalship.

18. Universal moral imperatives of leadership, such as a commitment to democracy and an ethic of caring, are not only possible but necessary.

As mentioned earlier, in point 14, yes.

19. Resolving moral dilemmas is easier over time and with experience.

It's rarely easy, but experience does provide you with perspective.

20. Although commonplace, ethical and moral dilemmas are challenging and require deep reflection about one's values and beliefs.

Most definitely. However, it is critical to keep in mind that rational and critical ethical thinking "that goes beyond personal beliefs and values" can help you lead a morally responsible life as a principal (Strike & Soltis, 1998, p. 5).

Reflective Questions

1. Which of the explanations above make the most sense to you?

2. Which of the explanations above make the least sense to you? Explain why.

3. Can you think of an instance when your personal values or ethics came into conflict with school or district policy? Explain how you resolved the dilemma.

4. Can anyone develop into an ethical leader? Explain why or why not.

5. Recall principals you know or have known and examine their ethical actions. Are they people you would want to emulate? Explain.

See Resource B for a more detailed survey to assess your ethical and spiritual self.

CHAPTER ONE

Introduction

"The work of educators differs from that of professionals in other fields in its opportunity to influence the holistic growth of persons and their communities. Teachers and administrators, on a daily basis and over an extended period of time, work with young people as they pass through their formative years. They have the privilege of creating environments where persons can learn and develop as healthy, moral, responsible, competent spouses, parents, workers, citizens, friends, and individuals. This is education. Anything less or different represents a reductionistic, bastardized understanding of our field."

—Lynn G. Beck

"Renewal is about the process of individual and organizational change, about nurturing the spiritual, affective, and intellectual connections in the lives of educators working together to understand and improve their practice."

—Kenneth A. Sirotnik

In the words of Elaine Wilmore (2002), "Being a leader is not an easy job" (p. 90). As principals, we are confronted with ethical and moral situations that challenge our sensibilities and, at times, frustrate us to the breaking point. This book is written as a basic primer to alert you to issues that are too often taken for granted and rarely addressed. A variety of options were available to me in framing this book. I could have taken a deeply philosophical approach that grappled with numerous ethical dilemmas without presenting a specific direction for practice. Such an approach, although intellectually satisfying, would not, in my estimation, provide you with more concrete information for practically serving in your role as principal. I could also have taken a detailed theoretical perspective by highlighting and reviewing the work of scholars such as Martin Buber (1965), David Hume (1983), Immanuel Kant (1966), Lawrence Kohlberg (1971), Friedrich Nietzsche (1973), and, more recently, Nel Noddings (2003). But again, I wanted to provide a more practical approach; besides, many other excellent works have been published in this area for you to consider. Another tactic would be to provide you with several approaches for resolving real-world ethical and moral dilemmas by working through varied case studies. The works of Maxcy (2002) and Strike, Haller, and Soltis (2005) are perhaps the best examples of this approach.

The approach taken in this book is to provide an introduction to ethical and spiritual ideas related to the principalship that is content rich, encourages reflection, and presents practical ideas for school leadership. The work is not morally neutral, in that I have a definite viewpoint and approach that I advocate. Still, you are encouraged to develop your own approach to the subject. The purpose of the book, then, is fourfold:

1. Review key ideas of ethical and spiritual leadership by highlighting best practices.

2. Highlight leadership virtues that I deem essential for school leadership.

3. Present various approaches to resolving ethical dilemmas.

4. Champion moral imperatives for school leadership.

Included throughout the book are reflection and self-assessment tools encouraging you to examine your ethical and spiritual leadership proclivities and interests.

* * * * * * * * * * * * * * * *

Ethics is not universal. What one principal may consider unethical, another may consider morally responsible. Like leadership, ethics is "not a neat and tidy concept," explain Komives and colleagues (1998, p. 264). Leading ethically and adhering to one's moral principles aren't easy. Life and leadership are complicated. As a principal, you should expect to be continually bombarded and confronted with dilemmas that aren't easily resolvable. As human beings, we are fallible; we make mistakes. Yet leading with conviction and integrity means making the tough choices even in the face of staunch opposition, personally and socially. We need principals with deep-seated convictions, a strong sense of morals, and an unwavering commitment to doing the right thing. As Komives and colleagues remind us, "leading with a moral purpose is central to the leadership process" (p. 271).

This work is also guided by eight assumptions of ethical leadership reviewed by Komives and colleagues (1998), citing Lucas and Anello (1995):

1. Ethics is the heart of leadership—leading with integrity.

2. All leadership is value driven—treating others justly and fairly.

3. The journey to ethical leadership begins with an examination of personal values—reflecting on one's core values. These values serve as moral compasses to guide decisions you make about ethical dilemmas you face.

4. Ethical leadership can be learned in a variety of ways—through personal experience, trial and error, reflection, and so on.

5. Ethical leadership involves a connection between ethical thought and action—what is necessary is not to learn many ethical theorists and philosophical works, but rather to engage in reflecting personal values applied to real ethical dilemmas.

6. Character development is an essential ingredient of ethical leadership—"walking the talk."

7. Members at all levels of an organization or community have the opportunity and responsibility to participate in

the process of exercising ethical leadership—all members of the school have a responsibility to act ethically and to advance core values of the school.

8. Everything we do teaches—we are role models, and our actions speak louder than our words.

Reflective Questions

1. Consider leaders you have known. Assess their ethical leadership skills. What stands out as particularly noteworthy? Unworthy?

2. Assess the ethical climate in your school. How can you contribute to a more ethical climate?

3. What ethical or moral challenges do you face? Explain.

4. React to the eight assumptions listed above. Which make the most sense to you?

---

* * * * * * * * * * * * * * * *

What can we say about spirituality? I wrote this book because I believe that leadership is a spiritual and intellectual calling. Leadership, like teaching, is both a science and an art. Many believe that principals are born great. Others maintain that one can become a great principal. Serving as principal affords you the opportunity to accomplish something special, to make a significant difference in the lives of many students, teachers, and others. Some educators value working only with students as a classroom teacher. Doing so is lofty and should be acknowledged and rewarded. Serving as principal, however, gives you the chance of making a difference on a larger scale. Many principals I have known care deeply about their work. They are involved in what Gary Zukav (2000) calls "sacred tasks." In his words,

Your sacred task is part of the agreement that your soul made with the Universe before you were born. When you are doing it, you are happy and fulfilled. You know that you are in a special and wonderful place. . . . When you are not doing your sacred task, you are miserable. (p. 241)

People have different sacred tasks. For some, starting a business might serve as a path for fulfillment; for others, it might be to raise a family, or to cook. For us, it is leading: inspiring, encouraging . . . touching another's soul . . . moving them to realization and understanding. As principals, we must recognize our sacred task. Never forget why you are a principal.

Reflective Questions

1. What does spiritual leadership mean to you?

2. How is serving as a principal a "sacred task"?

---

* * * * * * * * * * * * * * * *

The major themes or underlying assumptions of this book and series on the principalship are as follows:

- As principal, you model ethical behavior and base decisions on a moral grounding aligned to school and district values. You openly engage faculty, students, and community in discussions of ethical issues and moral dilemmas. You remain proactive by engaging in such conversations by reviewing school policies or ethical codes for behavior. However, you don't rely on these stated codes to perfunctorily dictate behavior. Rather, you encourage critical thinking, intellectual discourse, and critical reflection about pressing issues or situations as they arise. You encourage a learning community in which these ideas are encouraged and supported (Starratt, 2002).

- As principal, you maintain an unwavering moral commitment to high achievement for all students. You serve as a champion for the rights of all students to receive the highest-quality education possible. You encourage high-quality teaching and set high standards for performance, socially and academically. In this role, you champion justice, equality, and opportunity for all students, teachers, parents, and community members (Starratt, 2003).

• The principal must play an active, ongoing role in ethical leadership. The comprehensive study *Making Sense of Leading Schools: A Study of the School Principalship* (Portin, 2003) indicated that principals do not necessarily have to have expertise in all areas (e.g., instructional, cultural, managerial, human resources, strategic, external development, micropolitical leadership), but they must be master "diagnosticians," able to provide the school what it needs at the right time and in the right context. Nevertheless, I maintain that ethical leadership is qualitatively different from most other forms of leadership. Although it's difficult to separate each form of leadership from the others, because they all form an undifferentiated whole, ethical leadership can never be simply delegated to others. Every word you speak, every action you take shapes the ethical climate of your school. Others confront moral dilemmas and make ethical decisions, but you, as the principal, play a modeling role for the school community (Hopkins, 1997).

• The work you do as principal is spiritual in nature. Your work is buttressed by a firm set of values and beliefs about leadership. You act consistently on these beliefs. You are concerned with the growth of all people in your school—academically, socially, and emotionally. You realize that you prepare students for life, not just for school. You are people oriented and exhibit an ethic of caring and concern for all community members. You care deeply about assisting each person to achieve her or his potential. You provide a conducive learning community that fosters holistic learning and development. You value aesthetics; the arts; and commonly held values of trust, respect, and tolerance. Human values are at the center of

> "The principal is the 'high priest,' the one who seeks to define, strengthen, and articulate those enduring values, beliefs, and cultural strands that give the school its identity."
>
> —Thomas J. Sergiovanni

your work. You break through mundane daily routines and help others see possibilities for personal growth and hope for a better future and world. These and other similar ideas are of utmost concern for you, as spiritual leader (Gallegos Nava, 2001).

• The relationship between ethics and spirit is obvious to you. Promulgating ethical behavior and affirming moral commitment are spiritual imperatives, because they go to the very core of your work. They are what drives and sustains you. They are important; they make a difference.

This book and series are also aligned with standards established by the prominent Educational Leadership Constituent Council (ELCC). ELCC standards are commonly accepted by most educational organizations concerned with preparing high-quality educational leaders and as such are most authoritative (Wilmore, 2002). The ELCC, an arm of the National Council for the Accreditation of Teacher Education, developed six leadership standards used widely in principal preparation. These standards formed the basis for this book and series:

1.0: Candidates who complete the program are educational leaders who have the knowledge and ability to promote the success of all students by facilitating the development, articulation, implementation, and stewardship of a school or district vision of learning supported by the school community.

2.0: Candidates who complete the program are educational leaders who have the knowledge and ability to promote the success of all students by promoting a positive school culture, providing an effective instructional program, applying best practices to student learning, and designing comprehensive professional growth plans for staff.

3.0: Candidates who complete the program are educational leaders who have the knowledge and ability to promote the success of all students by managing the organization, operations, and resources in a way that promotes a safe, efficient, and effective learning environment.

4.0: Candidates who complete the program are educational leaders who have the knowledge and ability to promote the success of all students by collaborating with families and other community members, responding to diverse community interests and needs, and mobilizing community resources.

*5.0: Candidates who complete the program are educational leaders who have the knowledge and ability to promote the success of all students by acting with integrity, fairly, and in an ethical manner.

6.0: Candidates who complete the program are educational leaders who have the knowledge and ability to promote the success of all students by understanding, responding to, and influencing the larger political, social, economic, legal, and cultural context.

* This standard is addressed in this book.

Readers should also familiarize themselves with the Interstate School Leaders Licensure Consortium and National Association of Elementary School Principals standards (see, e.g., http://www.ccsso.org/projects/Interstate_School_Leaders_Licensure_Consortium/ and http://www.boyercenter.org/basicschool/naesp.shtml).

Another important point to make in this introduction is for you to realize that although with other forms of leadership (e.g., instructional, operational, and strategic) you must take specific actions to address them and at times you don't actually have to actively engage in them, as an ethical and spiritual leader you are continually affecting school culture and climate 24-7. Your daily activities, actions, memoranda, e-mails, personal contacts, decisions, and so forth reflect, shape, and influence school culture and climate.

> "One aspect of a student's moral education lies not in the curriculum but in the behavior of the faculty, staff, and administration and in the policies of the institution."
>
> —Harold T. Shapiro

Your actions as an ethical and spiritual leader are affirmed by these general core values (which are meant to serve as examples, not as an exhaustive list):

- Respect for the dignity of all persons
- Emphasis on an ethic of caring
- Belief in the power of education to transform lives
- Dedication to support educators as change agents
- Affirmation of social justice, equity, and educational opportunity
- Commitment to appreciating and celebrating diversity and cultural understanding among all people in a free, democratic society
- Belief that quality learning for all students depends on quality learning for all educators
- Development of the whole person
- Commitment to professional excellence, integrity, collegiality, and ethical behavior
- Support for a milieu that encourages intellectual curiosity, critical inquiry, and rational pedagogy
- Emphasis on a constructivist, hands-on approach to learning
- Belief in lifelong learning
- Dedication to making a difference in the academic and social lives of students

These general core values are actualized in your commitment to core values related specifically to leadership, as exemplified in these ideas:

- Strong leadership has the power to improve schools.
- Everyone is able to lead in some way to some degree in a given situation at some time.
- Leaders are not the same—leadership styles, personalities, or traits vary greatly.
- No one way of leading is better than another—each leader is talented in a different way.
- Effective leadership depends on the context—matching the right leader to a particular situation is most important.
- Building-level leadership is critical to improve teaching and promote student achievement.
- Effective organizations need all types of leaders—different leaders positioned strategically throughout a school or district can contribute greatly to organizational effectiveness.
- Effective leaders possess key virtues that mark who they are and what they care about.

Reflective Questions

1. Which of the themes or core values above make the most sense to you?

2. Which of the themes or core values above make the least sense to you? Explain.

3. How do you perceive your role as ethical and spiritual leader? What specific actions must you take to be effective?

4. What do you do on a daily basis that affirms your commitment to ethical and spiritual leadership? Provide details with examples.

---

* * * * * * * * * * * * * * *

Allow me to offer a word on chapter format and presentation of information. Information in each of the three main chapters is presented as concisely as possible to make for easy and quick reference reading. Each chapter begins with boxed material called "What You Should Know About." The box will list and briefly explain the concepts covered in each chapter. Certainly, each chapter will not cover every bit of information there is to know about a given topic, as mentioned earlier. Each chapter culls, though, essential knowledge, skills, and dispositions necessary for a successful principal.

A brief word on chapter organization is in order to facilitate reading. The second chapter includes some "best practices" for helping you create a sense of ethical behavior in your school, for developing a moral grounding in life in general, and for tapping into a spiritual dimension. After this introduction to some practical ideas of ethics, morality, and spirituality, the third chapter highlights five virtues for leading with a sense of spirit and ethics. The extent to which you actualize these virtues will determine your leadership success. The fourth chapter focuses on helping you address those thorny, practical ethical dilemmas you face on a daily basis. This book is not meant to be the definitive treatise on ethical and spiritual leadership, but rather to raise some relevant issues for your consideration. It is my hope that the ideas in this book will give you pause to think about your own sense of ethics in your interactions with others and encourage you to ponder the spiritual side of your work.

As a concluding activity to this Introduction, read the boxed material below, which contains 15 quotations meant to inspire, but also, and more important, to provoke critical thinking about your role as ethical or spiritual leader. Read each quotation and ask yourself these questions:

- What does the author convey about ethics or spirituality (in other words, what's the message in a nutshell)?
- Critique the quotation. Does the thought reflect your beliefs? Explain.
- What practical step(s) could you take to actualize the idea behind each quotation?

Some Key Quotations Related to Ethical and Spiritual Leadership

"I am assuming that to behave ethically is to behave under the guidance of an acceptable and justifiable account of what it means to be moral."

—Nel Noddings

"I use the word *soul* . . . to call for attention in schools to the inner life; to the depth dimension of human experience; to . . . longings for something more than an ordinary, material, and fragmented existence."

—Rachel Kessler

"We need heroes, people who can inspire us, help shape us morally, spur us on to purposeful action—and from time to time we are called on to *be* those heroes, leaders for others . . . we seem to need moral leadership especially, but the need for moral inspiration is ever present."

—Robert Coles

"Not everyone in an organization is prepared or willing to do the right thing or has a moral orientation. Some would prefer to take the easy way out, do what is more economical, or take the path of least resistance."

—Susan R. Komives, Nance Lucas, and
Timothy R. McMahon

"Being a school leader is not an easy job. In many ways, the moral and ethical decisions are the hardest ones we make. . . . The key is taking time to reflect and genuinely examine our behavior, our goals, our mission—and ourselves."

—Elaine L. Wilmore

"By clarifying personal beliefs about schooling and learning, resolving ethics issues, keeping physically and emotionally fit, reflecting on practice and continuing to grow professionally, the person who is becoming a principal will be able to carry out day to day duties and enjoy life. Nurturing the inner person is not easy, but it is imperative if the principal is to be truly successful and effective in helping the school learning community grow."

—Marsha Speck

"A moral way of being is a moral way of being human. Hence, one's morality will flow from one's humanity."

—Robert J. Starratt

"Even under the best of circumstances, leading in tomorrow's organization won't come easily. It will be a constant struggle resulting in large part from the changing conception of leadership. Each of the previous chapters captures a piece of the struggle and includes ideas for overcoming it. But there is one more piece that we haven't yet looked at. It is the difficulty of wrestling with paradox."

—Jerry L. Patterson

"Ethical thinking and decision making are not just following the rules."

—Kenneth Strike and Jonas F. Soltis

"The soul is where the inner and the outer world meet."

—Novalis

"Some people say that the universe is dead (they call it 'inert'), and that everything that happens is accidental (they say 'random'). Other people, like me, say that the Universe is alive, wise and compassionate. Looking at the universe as dead is one story. Looking at it as alive is another. Which story is true for you?"

—Gary Zukav

"Integrity is a fundamental consistency between one's values, goals, and actions."

—Robert Evans

"Leadership . . . involves opportunities to surface and mediate perceptions, values, beliefs, information, and assumptions through continuing conversations; to inquire about and generate ideas together; to seek to reflect upon and make sense of work in the light of shared beliefs and new information; and to create actions that grow out of these new understandings. Such is the core of leadership."

—Linda Lambert

"As a school leader, your ethical decisions are observed by others within the school—students, teachers, and staff. Your decisions affect these individuals and the school as a whole. The success or failure of the moral space of the school is affected by your moral and ethical leadership."

—Spencer J. Maxcy

"An abundance of caring is a signal quality found in most educators. This propensity to step outside of oneself, to see, hear, and appreciate another human being, increases insight, aids communication, and promotes excellence in instruction. Learners served by caring educators feel more important, demonstrate higher motivation, learn faster and better, and reveal greater confidence about their future. That is education as its best."

—Donald R. Draayer

CASE STUDY AND REFLECTIVE QUESTIONS

(The following case is modeled after Drake & Roe, 2003, pp. 35–36.)

It was a bright sunny morning as Jean Baptiste awoke from a deep sleep. His vacation was wonderful, and returning to work after such a respite was onerous. Jean had no idea what challenge awaited him as he returned to work, arriving at 5:45 a.m. Silver Lake High was a school located in a fairly conservative upper-middle-class neighborhood in a suburb of Wisconsin. Although the student body was primarily white, in recent years the numbers of people of color had increased, although they still made up less than 5% of the population. The Parent Teacher Association was always very active, surprisingly so for such a large high school. Such active participation was due primarily to the outreach and genuine sincerity of its principal. Well liked, gregarious, and diligent, Jean Baptiste had enjoyed his 4 years as principal of the high school. Although his first 2 years were difficult, because he had completely reorganized the traditional school scheduling to the blocked approach and had met with some opposition to his efforts, things had settled down recently. Teachers and students had become accustomed to the new routines. Teachers unwilling to deal with the change had transferred out of the school. The principal had attracted some new teachers trained in differentiated instruction and accustomed to block scheduling. Jean Baptiste had a reputation as a tough but fair-minded principal. This morning when he arrived, the school building seemed like any other, routine and uneventful . . . or so he thought.

Susan Neiman, one of the teachers, greeted Mr. Baptiste in his office. "Good morning, Susan. What brings you here so early this beautiful morning?" Anything but stoic, Susan nervously and anxiously alerted her principal to the impending controversy. "I don't think you are aware of the fact that several parents complained to me and some other teachers," she explained, "about Bill Smith and his committee's decision to honor gay history month. They intend to display material honoring gay history month on the bulletin board on the main floor near the school entrance. Some teachers also intend to post flyers and articles about gay issues in their classrooms."

"Well," reacted Mr. Baptiste, "it seems we have some time to speak to Bill and his committee about their decision."

Later that morning, Jean called Bill Smith into his office and asked him about the rumor he had heard about celebrating gay history month. "You know, Bill," explained Jean, "such a decision might not sit well with some parents here. We need to first discuss the issue as a faculty and as a parent-teacher association." Bill listened respectfully as the one-sided discussion ended. Bill did inform Jean that he would speak with committee members. Jean responded, "And please, Bill, report back to me."

The following Monday morning, Jean arrived at school to find a lavish bulletin board display in honor of gay history month. Disappointed that he was not consulted, he called Bill into his office to communicate his dissatisfaction. "I thought we had agreed that you'd report back to me."

"Well," explained Bill, "I don't recall saying that I promised to report back to you. I did meet with committee members, though, and we all felt that this issue needed immediate action without having to seek prior approval. It's a matter of justice and equality for gay rights."

Incensed with Bill's response, Mr. Baptiste ordered him to take down the display. "I'm not necessarily against honoring the month, but I am perturbed about the way you and your self-made committee went about implementing the event. I want the board taken down immediately, and I don't want teachers posting articles in their classrooms before we have a chance as a faculty to discuss the issue."

Bill stormed out of the office in defiance. Jean told the custodian to remove the display. As Jean crafted a memorandum to faculty on the issue, unbeknownst to him Bill called the superintendent, charging Mr. Baptiste with censorship. Several committee members later that day called the local newspaper to report the issue. Before long, the headline read "Controversy at Silver Lake High over Gay Rights."

The superintendent, the PTA, and the editorial column of the local newspaper support Mr. Baptiste's actions, explaining that "the school administration has the responsibility to uphold the integrity of the school" and that "all students, regardless of their background or orientation, should be accepted, and to highlight one particular lifestyle over another is unwarranted."

The controversy did not abate, however. Committee members reached out to several local politicians and even to the state Anti-Defamation League, which hired an attorney to support the committee's actions. Despite Mr. Baptiste's attempts to quell the controversy by conducting public forums on the issue, activists staunchly repeated their accusations of censorship by school and district leadership. Activists reiterated their message in forum after forum: "It's a matter of free speech and censorship. Besides, we have a moral obligation to obliterate antigay sentiments in this community. You can't mandate that gay-rights issues disappear."

At a closed-to-the-public parents' association session, one articulate parent rose and said, "Gays don't need a display to celebrate their history. Their subculture is a slap in the face to everything that is decent" (Drake & Roe, 2003, p. 36). She received thunderous applause from many participants.

Reflective Questions

1. What ethical issues are at stake in this case?

2. Do you as the principal have the right to order such displays removed?

3. Critique Mr. Baptiste's leadership in this case. What did or didn't he do correctly in your estimation?

4. How would you have reacted to this scenario? Be specific.

5. If you were the superintendent, what would you advise Mr. Baptiste to do next?

6. Assume parents keep demanding that Mr. Baptiste continue the ban on gay-rights displays and forums, and assume that he is in favor of such displays (although he disagreed with the way teachers went about the whole issue). How should Mr. Baptiste express his support of gay rights but at the same time engender parental support? Is such an attempt possible? Explain.

7. What other factors, not discussed, are implicated in this case?

8. How does the information presented in this book so far about ethical and spiritual leadership shed light on this case?

As mentioned in the Introduction, the next chapter builds upon the preceding information by highlighting some "best practices" for helping you create a sense of ethical behavior in your school, for developing a moral grounding in life in general, and for tapping into a spiritual dimension. These ideas are not meant to be exhaustive of the topic, but merely a means to encourage thinking about what it means to serve ethically, behave morally, and have a sense of the spiritual.

CHAPTER TWO

Best Practices in Leading Ethically, With Moral Purpose, and With an Awareness of the Spiritual

"Successful leadership and administrative practices depend largely on the principal's ethics. Honesty and ethical behaviors guide the principal's actions and demonstrate the sense of purpose and commitment that a school learning community expects from a principal. Thus, principals must be clear about their core beliefs to be consistent and fair in their daily actions in a school."

—Marsha Speck

"The quest for soul in education can move forward only in communities where educators, parents, and civic leaders are

> *willing to air their deepest differences in a spirit of dialogue and collaboration."*
>
> —Rachel Kessler

L eading is not easy. As leaders, we are expected to do much. Is it indeed possible to live up to the expectations of the title of this chapter? I think so. We certainly are not the sole exemplars of such virtues or responsibilities, but it is incumbent upon us to set an ethical, moral, and spiritual tone in our school building.

You will not be able to satisfy everyone with your decisions. Others may have strong differing opinions that may lead to resentment or dissatisfaction. Although you will certainly try to allay their apprehensions, you should realize that you cannot change everyone's opinion. "It's lonely at the top," as one of my mentors once posited.

Still, you should always strive to lead ethically, with moral purpose, and with spiritual awareness of your role as principal. "Be true to yourself" is another valuable lesson my mentor advised. Successful ethical and spiritual leaders ask themselves the following questions, among others:

- What are the beliefs and values that I would fight for?
- How might I best communicate beliefs and values to my faculty and staff?
- How do I reconcile differing beliefs and values with my own?
- How do I react in a crisis?
- Do I involve others in the decision-making process?
- Do I consider the perspective of the other?
- Am I caring and sensitive to others' feelings?
- Do I demonstrate by deed that I care?
- How do I know I'm doing a good job as a leader?

What can we say about ethics, morality, and spirituality? The term *ethics* comes from the Greek word *ethos*, meaning "character." *Moral* is derived from the Latin translation of ethics, *moris*, meaning "behavior." As one moves from ethics to morality, one moves from character to action. We can talk about ethics, but actions speak louder than words. The word *spirit,* on the other hand, comes from the Latin *spiritum,* meaning "nonmaterial."

How do these terms relate to one another? Acting ethically and morally (i.e., in word and deed) is indicative, in my view, of those who are in touch with their spiritual self or nature. People who behave unethically have low self-esteem and are inconsiderate of and inattentive to the needs of others. They also may have a warped sense of right and wrong. They tend to rationalize their actions easily, without guilt. They rarely think twice about their actions. Think about some famous people in the news who have been judged unethical, and see if the above descriptions, at least in part, don't ring true. On the other hand, someone who behaves ethically and follows her moral conscience is a deeply reflective, caring, and sensitive individual who is deeply considerate of others.

Reflective Questions

1. What kinds of situations do you encounter that call for mindful attention to ethical concerns?

2. What other kinds of questions do ethical and spiritual leaders ask themselves?

3. What other kinds of relationships are possible between ethical behavior and attentiveness to the spiritual?

4. Consider leaders you know and describe how they approach ethical decision making. What do they do that stands out in your mind? Would you call them spiritual people as well? Explain why or why not.

The following boxed material summarizes the teaching ideas highlighted in this chapter. The list is not exhaustive but is meant merely to highlight some key concepts and ideas that successful ethical leaders should know about as they go about their work creating an ethical tone for their buildings. Brief reflective activities follow each major concept to provoke thought on ways to implement or to further understand each idea.

What You Should Know About Leading Ethically, With Moral Purpose, and With an Awareness of the Spiritual

- **Maintaining Assumptions About Ethics**—We review some ideas about ethical and moral principles by Zubay and Soltis (2005).
- **Creating and Sustaining an Ethical Organization**—We review Nash's (1990) four qualities for doing so.
- **Affirming Three Qualities for a Moral Life**—We review Starratt's (1996) three qualities for doing so.
- **Following Seven Spiritual Gateways**—We review Kessler's (2000) seven gateways for enhancing the spiritual.
- **Becoming a Holistic Educator**—We review Gallegos Nava's (2001) ideas for becoming holistic.

---

1. MAINTAINING ASSUMPTIONS ABOUT ETHICS

We don't think and talk enough about ethics, especially about the degree to which we model acceptable ethical and moral behaviors. The study of ethics should be something we attend to in a serious, consistent way. Zubay and Soltis (2005) outline some of the following assumptions that we need to consider, as best practice, as we dialogue about ethics.

- Our personal and school cultures inform our ethical and moral principles. In other words, we learn how to behave ethically or morally from our culture. I recall an instance as a school administrator when I notified a parent that her child had punched another boy in the face, causing severe swelling. She responded, "Yes, I know; he told me the other boy pushed him first. I tell my boys that if someone harms you in some way, then you must take him out." Of course, I explained to this mother the import of matching personal codes of behavior with school policies, and so on.

- Decision making about moral dilemmas is enhanced through ethical reasoning. To the degree to which we think and reflect about how we might respond to a situation or event that addresses a moral issue, we will be in a better position to make a more reasoned and thoughtful decision. In other words, we get better at making ethical choices or decisions as we engage thoughtfully in critical thinking and reasoning. This process can occur before or after a decision is made.

- Related to this last point is the notion that ethical reasoning is a "skill that is acquired through practice" (Zubay & Soltis, 2005, p. 10). We get better at ethical decision making as we continue to reflect, make our decision, and reflect some more. Zubay and Soltis add, "Ethical reasoning is a skill that needs to be cultivated" (p. 18). Such cultivation can occur through analyzing case studies or situations that require ethical decision making (see Resource A, "Realities of Ethical and Spiritual Leadership"), but it's best arrived at through reflection on the job or, as Schon (1987) says, "reflection in and on action."

- We play a key role in shaping and influencing the ethical and moral choices of others, including teachers and students, by our own beliefs and actions. Allow me to relate a simplistic example of how we are influenced even unconsciously by the moral choices of others. I was a young student, perhaps a third grader, when I was sitting in the rear of the classroom as my teacher was hanging up his jacket in the closet. I was watching him in an early-morning, almost hypnotic trance. He inadvertently caused one of the empty hangers to fall to the floor. As he took one step away, he heard the clang of the hanger hitting the floor. He stopped, turned around, and placed the hanger back onto the rod in the closet. You know, to this day, whenever I accidentally cause a hanger to drop, I always pick it up. Why? Not because I have some sort of hanger fetish . . . ha . . . but because it was, and still is, the right thing to do.

- The school community should purposely seek to identify and agree upon common moral values. Devising some sort of code of ethics is less important than the process we engage in with the school community in thinking and discussing moral and ethical issues that might arise and how to deal with them as a community of learners. Zubay and Soltis (2005) explain that we need to engage others in "moral conversations, and thereby see that ethics is an important part of everyone's education" (p. 18).

- Articulate your own moral principles, and engage others in justifying actions taken based upon personal and school ethics.

- Other people have very different ways of seeing the same problem. Assume that you always need to see the other person's perspective.

- Ethical disagreements are normal. There is not always a best solution. Zubay and Soltis (2005), though, indicate that "some solutions are better and more just than others" (p. 18).

Reflective Question

1. On this last point, how do you know or determine which solution is better and more just?

---

2. CREATING AND SUSTAINING AN ETHICAL ORGANIZATION

Aside from behaving ethically and morally as an individual, a principal must be able to facilitate an ethical organization. Nash (1990) identifies four qualities for creating and sustaining an ethical organization:

> "If we could teach our students to care about important social problems and think about them rigorously, then clearly our institutions of learning must set a high example in the conduct of their own affairs."
>
> —Derek Bok

1. *Critical thinking skills, which assist an individual to weigh facts and draw conclusions about a given problem or dilemma.* Ethical behavior is fostered through critical thinking. Create a Think Tank composed of individuals who think creatively, out of the proverbial box. Brainstorm solutions to dilemmas or problems. Use consensus-building strategies.

2. *Personal integrity to stand up against opposing forces that go against personal or professional ethics.* Examine our discussion of courage in Chapter 3. Many principals are conservative and are fearful of confronting controversial issues. Reexamine your beliefs and values, and ask, "Will I do almost anything to remain true to them?"

3. *Looking at situations in a multidimensional way by seeing things from a variety of perspectives.* By training ourselves to think and see globally, we are better able to understand different ways of solving problems. Examining an educational problem sociologically, legally, psychologically, culturally, philosophically, economically, and politically gives us a broad understanding from which to generate possible solutions.

4. *Personal motivation to do the right thing.* As we said earlier, leadership is about doing the right things, not just doing things right. Affirm your commitment daily to "doing the right thing" by asking, "Am I doing the right thing in this situation?" Confirm your conclusions with a mentor or superior you respect.

Reflective Question

1. How do you create and sustain an ethical organization in your school? Provide a detailed description.

---

3. AFFIRMING THREE QUALITIES FOR A MORAL LIFE

Living and leading with moral purpose doesn't occur naturally. As principal, you must consciously decide to lead morally. According to Starratt (1996), "A moral way of being is a moral way of being human. Hence, one's morality will flow from one's humanity." He continues, stating that the "three qualities of a fully human person are *autonomy, connectedness,* and *transcendence*" (p. 157).

1. *Being autonomous*—As principal, you must realize that you are responsible for your choices and decisions. Although you consider the cultural and social context of your school, the moral choices you make set the tone for your school.

2. *Being connected*—As principal, you also realize that although you are an autonomous human being, no man [*sic*] is an island to himself. You are part of a community of others, and as such, you share, learn, and grow from and with others. You are morally (and spiritually) connected to relationships. You share cultural values and beliefs of humane treatment of other human beings.

3. *Being transcendent*—As principal, you realize your transcendent nature in the sense that you aspire to something greater than yourself. You strive to reach your potential, or you align yourself with community activism about some pressing social issue.

According to Starratt (1996), these "qualities are foundational in a developing ethical person" (p. 158). He encourages administrators to encourage "teachers throughout the school to design explicit learning activities which will involve the developing of these foundational qualities" (p. 159).

Reflective Questions

1. How are these three qualities interrelated?
2. How is transcendence related to spirituality?
3. How might you nurture a sense of transcendence in teachers?
4. How might you actualize these qualities in your school?

---

4. FOLLOWING SEVEN SPIRITUAL GATEWAYS

Principals can play a key role in addressing the spiritual needs of their faculty. Based on Kessler's (2000) seven categories, which she calls "gateways," you can guide your faculty to spiritual heights. The seven gateways are as follows:

- *The yearning for deep connection*—Each person has an innate desire for connecting with others in deep, meaningful social relationships. Each of us is part of a group; we're social animals, so to speak. Use that knowledge in your interactions with faculty. Also, each of us yearns to be connected to something larger and more enduring, such as a cause of some sort.

- *The longing for silence and solitude*—All of us need rest, rejuvenation of sorts. Aside from the proverbial vacation, you can foster time for critical reflection. Keep in mind Gateway 1, and have groups of individuals spend school-day time reflecting on some project idea or relevant issue.

- *The search for meaning and purpose*—At least consciously, educators do not always perceive their work in school as a spiritual enterprise, nor do they overtly wax philosophical. Still, all of us seek something beyond the mundane (e.g., "it's just a job"). Challenge teachers, for instance, to examine personal goals connected in some way to their professional "job." What are their purposes, their objectives, and what do they want for their students and school?

- *The hunger for joy and delight*—All of us want to have fun. Is working in your school fun? Certainly, we can't compare a vacation in the Bahamas to our job, but have we as principals established a warm, conducive atmosphere in which teachers, students, and parents feel welcome and safe? Are there fun activities, celebrations, parties, and so on?

- *The creative drive*—Do we nurture a spirit of creativity? Do we welcome new ideas or new ways of doing things? Do students and teachers have opportunities to share new thoughts or ideas? Can they experiment? According to Sousa (2003), who discusses these gateways, "This gateway is the most familiar for nourishing the spirit in school and is part of all the other gateways" (p. 218).

- *The urge for transcendence*—All of us have a desire, conscious or not, to experience something beyond the usual or the mundane. As human beings, we strive for excellence. Few people say, "I strive for mediocrity." You can encourage transcendence by supporting faculty and student interests in the arts, academics, sports, and so forth.

- *The need for initiation*—All people need acknowledgment for their efforts. You can acknowledge new teachers and students in your school; you can organize assembly programs for specific ceremonies, such as to initiate faculty or students into honor societies; and so on.

Reflective Questions

1. How might we encourage each of the gateways in our school? Provide specific strategies.

2. What other concrete ideas do you have for nurturing the spirit of students, faculty, and parents?

---

5. BECOMING A HOLISTIC EDUCATOR

Holistic educators consider their ethical behavior and spiritual nature as one. They understand and see the interrelationships among all things and beings. They are sensitive to the needs of the individual. In fact, they do not ask, "How can the individual conform to the exigencies of the organization?" Rather, they expect that the organization should meet individual needs and interests.

Gallegos Nava (2001) has written a cogent analysis of holistic education in which he articulates a vision and mission for a holistic educator. He contrasts the holistic educator with what he terms the *mechanistic educator* in the following ways, among others. Whereas the mechanistic educator provides knowledge, the holistic one creates learning contexts. Mechanistic educators promote competitive values, but the holistic educator encourages human values. Holistic educators aim to integrate knowledge; see the individual as a human being; and encourage dialogue, critical thinking, and problem solving.

Reflective Questions

1. How do these ideas address ethics and spirituality?

2. How might you actualize Gallegos Nava's ideas in your school in a practical way?

---

3. Describe principals you know who operate in mechanistic ways. Can you describe holistic educators you've seen in practice, even though they may not be called such? Explain.

CONCLUSION

Clearly, this subject is vast, and I have not covered all there is to know. Yet if you integrate the ideas in this chapter in some concrete ways, you'll at least be heading in the right direction.

Leading ethically, with moral purpose, and with an awareness of the spiritual is not easy, as we stated at the outset of this chapter, but it is nonetheless imperative. You may follow the advice given in this chapter, but if you have not fully integrated a sense of ethics and spirit into your personality, you will make a difficult process even more difficult. Use the questionnaires below as a means to gauge your sensitivities and sensibilities to ethics and spirit, and then read Chapter 3.

RESPOND #1

SA = Strongly Agree ("For the most part, yes.")
A = Agree ("Yes, but . . .")
D = Disagree ("No, but . . .")
SD = Strongly Disagree ("For the most part, no.")

SA A D SD 1. I get asked for help a lot, and I have a hard time saying no.

SA A D SD 2. When I meet a person, I'll give that individual the benefit of the doubt; in other words, I'll like the person until he or she gives me a reason not to.

SA A D SD 3. People usually like me.

SA A D SD 4. I'm happiest interacting with people and aiding them in some way.

(Continued)

SA   A   D   SD   5. People tell me I have a great sense
of humor.

SA   A   D   SD   6. I'm good at smoothing over others'
conflicts and helping to mediate them.

SA   A   D   SD   7. I believe that respect for authority is one
of the cornerstones of good character.

SA   A   D   SD   8. I feel I'm good at supervising a small
group of people, and I enjoy doing so.

SA   A   D   SD   9. I want my life to mean something.

SA   A   D   SD   10. I am more spiritual than most of my
friends.

Analyzing your responses:

Note that the items (above and below) are drawn from one of my previous books, *Finding Your Leadership Style: A Guide for Educators,* published by the Association for Supervision and Curriculum Development (Glanz, 2002). For a more detailed analysis, please refer to that work. Suffice it to say here that if you answered SA or A to the items above, you are a person who is dynamic in social settings and supportive of others. You are also likely ethical and spiritually sensitive. Of course, don't allow any one survey to sway you one way or another, but effective leaders, generally, are naturally inclined to help others; are caring, sensitive individuals; and possess a strong desire to make a difference.

RESPOND #2

(Responses are discussed after the questionnaire.)
SA = Strongly Agree ("For the most part, yes.")
 A = Agree ("Yes, but . . .")
 D = Disagree ("No, but . . .")
SD = Strongly Disagree ("For the most part, no.")

SA   A   D   SD   1. I acknowledge another point of view when
data indicate that the other's position is
more accurate.

SA   A   D   SD   2. When I make up my mind about an important educational issue or matter, I easily alter my stance if presented with information contrary to my stance.

SA   A   D   SD   3. In making decisions, I can absorb varied positions and pieces of evidence, and I usually remain neutral before I render my final decision, even in cases in which I may have vested interests.

SA   A   D   SD   4. Despite natural inclinations, I would not favor someone from my own ethnic group in rendering a decision about an educational matter.

SA   A   D   SD   5. I am not stubbornly close-minded when I know I am right.

SA   A   D   SD   6. I do not consciously make prejudgments about people.

SA   A   D   SD   7. I am usually consulted because people consider me fair and nonjudgmental.

SA   A   D   SD   8. I value honesty in words and action, and I have an unwavering commitment to ethical conduct.

Good principals are impartial. *Impartiality* is defined in this context as behavior that is free from prejudice and bias, such that no one individual is favored over another. Bias undermines good leadership because it interferes with an impartial review of information and people. It clouds our judgment. Let's examine your responses to the questionnaire above. The eight statements indicate your proclivity to act impartially as a leader. Each of these statements clearly provides an example of an impartial leader. Analyze each statement to better understand the extent to which you possess this character trait.

1. I acknowledge another point of view when data indicate that the other's position is more accurate.

(Continued)

A paradigm is a lens that affects what we perceive and how we interpret meaning. All of us view and understand the world through our lens. People in the 16th century, for instance, believed the earth was the center of the universe. They understood the world through an inaccurate paradigm. Galileo advocated a Copernican theory that suggested that the sun, not the earth, was at the center. Galileo, as you know, was threatened with torture to change his position. Certainly, we don't confront such onerous challenges, but we too suffer from *paradigm inflexibility,* which is the refusal or inability to accept alternate points of view.

2. When I make up my mind about an important educational issue or matter, I easily alter my stance if presented with information contrary to my stance.
Open-mindedness is the willingness to entertain alternate viewpoints. Can we change our minds whenever there is good reason to do so? Open-mindedness doesn't represent an "anything goes" attitude. Rather, it entails the willingness to critically examine different possibilities and presupposes a measure of tolerance. An impartial leader shows intellectual respect for others and their opinions.

3. In making decisions, I can absorb varied positions and pieces of evidence, and I usually remain neutral before I render my final decision, even in cases in which I may have vested interests.
Ask yourself, "What are my vested interests?" "If I had a vested interest in seeing a program implemented, for instance, could I or would I remain neutral to opposing viewpoints?" "Do I have paradigm flexibility, that is, the ability to consider multiple perspectives?"

4. Despite natural inclinations, I would not favor someone from my own ethnic group in rendering a decision about an educational matter.
Feeling comfortable around those who are like us is natural. When I enter a reception area at a conference where I don't know anyone, for example, I will tend to gravitate to people most like myself (for me, that's white, male, and Jewish). Such behavior is normal. However, I must remain vigilant not to favor others simply because they are very much like me. Rendering decisions as

educational leaders must not entail gender, religious, sexual, social, or racial bias.

5. I am not stubbornly close-minded when I know I am right.

Open-mindedness is easier when one is undecided or uncertain about a particular issue. Let's say you feel you are right about something. Can you still maintain an open-minded stance? An impartial educational principal can.

6. I do not consciously make prejudgments about people.

The key word is *consciously.* As human beings, it is normal to prejudge someone, for example. You meet someone for the first time, and you will inevitably, without intention to do so, observe the person's dress, manner of speech, and physical appearance. These stimuli will automatically register. Impartial leaders are aware of such reactions, acknowledge them, and purposely counter them in order to remain open-minded.

7. I am usually consulted because people consider me fair and nonjudgmental.

Do people consider you fair and nonjudgmental? Ask a colleague or two.

8. I value honesty in words and action, and I have an unwavering commitment to ethical conduct.

What have you done recently that would confirm such honesty and commitment to ethical conduct? Be specific. If you have difficulty coming up with an instance or two, then perhaps you are not as committed to these ideals as you might think.

Are you impartial?

RESPOND #3

(Responses are discussed after the questionnaire.)
SA = Strongly Agree ("For the most part, yes.")
 A = Agree ("Yes, but . . .")
 D = Disagree ("No, but . . .")
SD = Strongly Disagree ("For the most part, no.")

SA A D SD 1. When I hear about another's suffering, I am emotionally moved.

(Continued)

SA   A   D   SD   2. I demonstrate my compassion toward others (not part of my immediate family) by truly offering assistance, even going out of my way to do so.

SA   A   D   SD   3. I often think or meditate about the welfare of others and wish them the best of luck.

SA   A   D   SD   4. I would give friends the "shirt off my back" to assist them.

SA   A   D   SD   5. I value commitment to the development of the individual within the school and district, and I value treating all individuals as significant stakeholders in the organization.

SA   A   D   SD   6. Others would characterize me as a person who is kind, caring, nurturing, and sensitive.

SA   A   D   SD   7. I openly give recognition for outstanding professional performance because I sincerely want to acknowledge the contributions of others.

SA   A   D   SD   8. I am responsive and sensitive to the social and economic conditions of students, as well as to their racial, ethnic, and cultural backgrounds.

Good principals, in my view, are empathetic. Why is empathy such a vital virtue? If you have empathy, you have compassion for others. Caring for others communicates that they are important, worthwhile, and esteemed individuals. Treating people with such compassion will encourage them to respond in kind, to you and to others. Such behavior inspires them to do their utmost to help others.

1. When I hear about another's suffering, I am emotionally moved.
    Are you so immune to others' tragedies that you no longer are emotionally concerned? Empathetic people are not merely

intellectually aroused by the sufferings experienced by others. They "feel" their pain. Can you relate a time when you felt that way?

2. I demonstrate my compassion toward others (not part of my immediate family) by truly offering assistance, even going out of my way to do so.

Empathy may entail just listening to another's travail. A higher level of empathy is actually doing something to assist that person. Empathetic people don't hesitate to go out of their way to do so. When was the last time you went out of your way to help someone in a school situation?

3. I often think or meditate about the welfare of others and wish them the best of luck.

Empathetic people don't feel pity or sorrow for someone. Sympathetic people do that. Empathetic people think and, if they are religious, pray for others.

4. I would give friends the "shirt off my back" to assist them.

Empathetic people are doers.

5. I value commitment to the development of the individual within the school and district, and I value treating all individuals as significant stakeholders in the organization.

Empathetic people are people oriented and treat all people (custodians, teachers, students, parents, and colleagues) with kindness, benevolence, and goodwill.

6. Others would characterize me as a person who is kind, caring, nurturing, and sensitive.

This is the definition of an empathetic person.

7. I openly give recognition for outstanding professional performance because I sincerely want to acknowledge the contributions of others.

Empathetic leaders care for people by recognizing and rewarding their achievements. They do so not because it is required, but because they feel it is the right thing to do.

(Continued)

> *8. I am responsive and sensitive to the social and economic conditions of students, as well as to their racial, ethnic, and cultural backgrounds.*
>
> Empathetic leaders are concerned about all facets of peoples' lives and the conditions that affect them.
>
> Are you empathetic?

After this introduction to some practical ideas of ethics, morality, and spirituality, the third chapter will highlight five virtues, based on the work of Hare (1993), for leading with a sense of spirit and ethics. The extent to which you actualize these virtues will determine your success as a leader.

CHAPTER THREE

Leading With Soul and Conviction

Five Essential Virtues
for Effective Leadership

"For organizations . . . soul is a bedrock sense of who we are, what we care about, and what we believe in."

—Lee G. Bolman and Terrence E. Deal

"I have attempted to go beyond the concepts of leading with heart, soul, and morals and have moved on to the concept of love in an attempt to reteach the lessons of history's great leaders that can renew organizations."

—John R. Hoyle

"The job of the school is to provide students with knowledge and skills and to build character and instill virtue."

—Thomas J. Sergiovanni

I adhere to a branch of the study of ethics known as prescriptive or normative ethics. Someone who holds such a position is not morally neutral. According to Hopkins (1997), normative ethics "is concerned with the formulation of moral norms governing moral life and setting forth particular sets of standards that [are] best for people to adhere to" (p. 24). From my review of the literature about the principalship and my years of experience, I have found the ethical stances or virtues eluci-dated in this chapter to be particularly important and relevant to our work as principals. To be sure, others have identified different sets of virtues (e.g., Starratt, 1996). Mine are not, therefore, meant to serve as definitive virtues or leadership dispositions, but simply as suggestions to guide our work with a sense of moral grounding and spiritual sensitivity. Principals lead with soul and conviction, in my view, when they exhibit a set of ethical virtues that, based on Hare (1993), I call "five excellences."

What do I mean by "leading with *soul*"? Following Bolman and Deal's (1997) lead, I define *soul* as a bedrock sense of what we believe in, what we care about, and who we really are as individu-als. A leader with a sense of *soul* possesses a well-defined value system and a deep sense of self (Hoyle, 2002). Soulful leaders are aware of their unique qualities that make them particularly effec-tive as leaders. Conversely, they are aware of their limitations. My argument in this chapter is that who we are greatly influences our success as leaders. I certainly acknowledge the multifaceted con-textual, interpersonal, and political factors that influence leader-ship in schools. Yet we must not overlook the enormous influence of the individual to effect desired changes in schools. Current whole-school reform efforts especially, it seems to me, neglect the significant role of individual influence and human capacity to influence change (Elmore, 2000). This chapter focuses on the influence of the individual, personifying virtues, as most critical in terms of successful leadership.

Now, what do I mean by "leading with *conviction*"? Following Hare's (1993) lead, I maintain that leaders must possess essential characteristics, "virtues" (according to Hare) or, as I sometimes prefer to call them, "excellences."

A word about the selection of these virtues is in order. You will notice that "intelligence" or "competence" is not included. These abilities are essential, but they are a given. So, too, are descriptors such as "ethical" or "moral," which cannot, by the way, be easily defined and understood by all people. What may be ethical to one person may be scandalous to another. Still, the point is that someone who exemplifies these five virtues (based on Hare's 1993 work) will necessarily embody competence and intelligence and will likely display ethical or moral behavior. Besides, ethics and moral conduct are included, to a large degree, under the virtue of "judgment" (see below).

**What You Should Know About
Leading With Soul and Conviction**

- **Exhibiting Courage**—Principals remain steadfast in their beliefs and thus exhibit moral fortitude.
- **Maintaining Impartiality**—Principals commit to maintain a nonpartisan, unbiased position.
- **Demonstrating Empathy**—Principals identify with and feel another's pain.
- **Judging Ethically**—Principals are good decision makers because they weigh evidence fairly.
- **Remaining Humble**—Principals are aware of their limitations but at the same time are cognizant of their abilities.

Each of the best practices that follow offers insights into personal virtues that are essential for sound leadership as a principal.

1. EXHIBITING COURAGE

What does it mean to be a courageous leader? The word *courage* conjures up military motifs, such as heroic acts, daring exploits, and dramatic displays of fearlessness. What do bravery, gallantry, and valor have to do with educational leadership? Are there really inspiring acts of heroism displayed by leaders in schools? Why does a leader have to personify courage to be considered a good principal?

Although many forms of courage exist (e.g., physical, mental, or moral), the kind of courage necessary for principals is the willingness to stand up despite opposition. What is needed is the courage to speak out despite the constraining, formidable forces that are ever-present and serve to stifle individual initiative. The forces that urge, if not compel, conformity to the status quo are certainly substantial. However, to remain subservient to those individuals in positions of power and authority, or even to people who aggressively argue their position, in most cases wrongly, is anathema. To be courageous as a matter of principle should be valued and affirmed. By showing oneself to be principled, one displays immense strength of character. It is this strength of character that we call *courage*. We need principals who will gallantly assume responsibility for ensuring that the rights and dignities of others, especially the disenfranchised, are recognized and upheld. Speaking out against injustices such as unfair tracking placements, racist practices, and homophobic attitudes are just a few examples of courageous behaviors.

> *"Courage is leadership affirmed."*
>
> —Erik Erikson

These aforementioned examples of courage are the manifest ones. Principals also display courage in less visible ways. On a daily basis, leaders are expected to display more subtle forms of courage—the courage to do what others prefer not to do, the courage to confront difficult and uncomfortable situations, the courage to remain steadfast in one's beliefs.

Principals on a daily basis may not exhibit physical bravery (e.g., confronting a knife-wielding assailant), but every day they have to affirm their beliefs about what is most educationally sound. Leadership is not about performing administrative tasks such as assigning lunch duties, filing reports, or reviewing teacher lesson plans. These are the necessary but perfunctory duties principals may perform. Courage, however, comes into play when one's beliefs and attitudes about teaching, learning, students, supervision, and schools are called into question. Remaining faithful to one's educational and moral principles is what courage is all about.

A courageous principal, therefore, should have a well-reasoned, articulated belief system that supports and affirms the rights and dignities of all learners, of all people. In this sense, then, courage is integral to the effectiveness of a principal leader.

Why is courage such a vital virtue? Without courage, principals become mere technicians, administrative guardians, nothing more than custodians of the institution. Leading is about making the right decisions to benefit students, parents, and community. Schools are confronted by a plethora of demands that require principals to remain steadfast to their beliefs that support, most fundamentally, student learning. Courage to stand up for what is right will safeguard the beliefs we hold so dear and true. *Courage,* then, is defined as the ability to stand behind one's principles, thus displaying immense strength of character.

As a principal you can best actualize your role as a courageous leader if you:

• *Articulate your beliefs*—Studies demonstrate that people with firm beliefs are more courageous than those who act impulsively. Critically examining your ideals and values and then forming a belief system will serve as a bedrock to rely upon when confronted with a crisis that threatens the beliefs you hold dear and true (Osterman & Kottkamp, 2004).

• *Role-play situations that require courage*—As hokey as this suggestion may sound, acting out a response to a situation before it transpires will fortify you. Imagine, for instance, standing up to Mrs. Kessle, an irate parent who continually storms into your office and demands your time. This is admittedly a simple example for which courage may be needed, but nonetheless, it's a good way to start. Close your eyes and imagine this parent entering your office. What can you say to her to communicate your desire that she call for an appointment in the future? Try to say something without sounding rude and disrespectful. You might say, "Mrs. Kessle, I'd like to see you, but this is a bad time. I must attend a meeting with a teacher. I will call you later to set up an appointment to discuss your concerns." If she insists on seeing you now, don't falter. Use the "broken-record" technique. Restate your position firmly while maintaining eye contact. "I understand that you want to speak with me, but this is not a good time." Once successful, by the way, you will gain the confidence to display similar degrees of courageousness (even more so) in the future. Recall what Aristotle once said: "We become brave by doing brave acts."

Reflective Question

1. Assess your personal degree of courage. In what instances
   were you courageous, or less so?

---

2. MAINTAINING IMPARTIALITY

What does it mean to be an impartial leader? The word *impartial*
may conjure up images of umpires at baseball games or judges
weighing evidence at trials. Whether an umpire or judge, these
individuals make decisions by weighing evidence presented to
them, considering the evidence from the perspective of a prescribed set of rules, and rendering decisions after deliberation.
Although baseball umpires have to render decisions instanta-
neously, whereas judges may benefit from increased time for deliberation, both individuals are presumed to have based their
judgments on fair, unbiased assessments, to the best of their ability. What does impartiality have to do with educational leadership? Is it really possible for a principal to assume an impartial
stance when dealing with complex issues involving students,
parents, educators, and the community? Why does a leader have
to personify impartiality to be considered a good principal?

Impartiality is defined in this context as behavior that is free
from prejudice and bias, in which no one individual is favored over
another. Bias undermines leadership because it interferes with an
impartial review of evidence and argument. If our approach is
biased, we fail to do justice to those who rely on our judgments as
leaders. If we are biased, we are inclined to accept some positions
or accounts more readily than others. Take a situation in which a
principal is confronted by a wealthy and well-known parent in the
community whose son is charged with a crime that warrants sus-
pension from the school. The parent pleads with you in private,
stating that he would greatly appreciate "consideration in this
matter." We can readily see the connection between various
virtues. It may take courage to withstand the requests of this
father. But are there alternatives? Can we as committed principals
abrogate our responsibility to treat all our people equitably and
justly? By showing partiality to a child whose parent is well placed

in the community, aren't we performing an injustice to another child whose parent is less favorably positioned? Favoritism leads inevitably to corruption. Principals must be committed to fairly assessing all relevant evidence and must strive to be immune to the personal or social pressures that may come to bear, thus rendering an unbiased decision.

Does impartiality mean we are neutral? Neutrality may indeed be difficult, if not impossible. No person can be prejudice free. Our biases run deep. They have been culturally and socially engrained, reinforced by family and peer pressures. We are often immune to how they operate, how they shape what we see, and how we interpret meaning. As human beings, we are bound by our perspectives, our unique vantage points. Reality is seen and understood by our belief systems, which are in turn based on assumptions gleaned from our experiences. Reality is dependent on our thinking patterns, belief systems, and mind-sets. Our belief systems are very much connected to the language we use to communicate meanings, which influence our actions and behaviors. How we think shapes the world in which we live. As Arthur Schopenhauer once stated, "The world in which a man lives shapes itself chiefly by the way in which he looks at it." Learning to be impartial means we are cognizant of our biases, prejudices, and predispositions. Principals should be impartial, and where they know they are strongly committed to a viewpoint, they must do everything possible to compensate for their bias by giving alternative views a fair hearing and representation.

Impartiality, however, is more than assuming a bias-free disposition. Although awareness is certainly critical, principals are charged with the responsibility of taking action to combat, for instance, prejudice, discrimination, hate, and injustice.

Good principals understand the import of maintaining a bias-free attitude that includes, for instance, following a judicious and impartial review of all relevant evidence in all cases and not simply proceeding from a partisan position, holding onto certain views dogmatically. Awareness of bias and action to combat it are not only possible but necessary in our diverse, multiethnic, multiracial society. In this sense, then, impartiality is integral to the effectiveness of a principal.

Why is impartiality such a vital virtue? Without maintaining an impartial stance, we conduct our affairs based on unexamined assumptions. Although all human behavior is fundamentally subjective and selective, a principal who intentionally considers options, explores alternate ways of thinking and behaving, and promotes equity for all people affirms and facilitates an educational environment conducive to learning and achievement for all. *Impartiality*, then, is defined as the commitment to maintaining a nonpartisan position in regard to issues and taking an active stand against hate, bias, and all injustices.

As a principal, you can best actualize your role as an impartial leader if you engage in the following actions:

• *Examine your own biases.* The word *prejudice*, derived from the Latin noun *praejudicium*, originally meant "precedent"—a judgment based on previous decisions and experiences. Later, the word came to mean a judgment formed before examining and considering all the facts. It is not easy to say how much fact is required in order to justify a judgment. A prejudiced person will say she or he has sufficiently considered all the facts to warrant a viewpoint. She or he may then relate all the negative experiences she or he has had with Catholics, Jews, Irish, Hispanics, and so forth. Examining one's biases presupposes the understanding that everyone is prejudiced to some degree; that is, everyone sometimes makes prejudgments about people and in situations. "Are all or most women poor drivers?" "Do all or most Asians excel in math and science?" "Are all or most Jews interested in making money?" "Are all or most African American students low achievers?" What are your prejudices? How do you know? What do you do to ensure that they don't affect your decisions as a principal? (Allport, 1987).

• *Take action to combat bias.* Impartiality in this chapter has been explained as more than assuming a neutral stance. Taking *action* to combat oppression is an important responsibility of a principal. What action have you recently taken to demonstrate your impartiality?

• *Confront curricular bias.* Although textbooks over the past 10 years have improved in terms of ensuring nonracist and non-sexist books, problems still persist. Consider these seven forms of bias that may exist in various instructional materials (see, e.g., Zittleman & Sadker, n.d.):

* *Invisibility:* Do the materials, for example, omit African Americans, Latinos, and Asian Americans?

* *Stereotyping:* Do the materials, for example, portray only dynamically aggressive men?

* *Imbalance and Selectivity:* Do the materials, for example, make reference only to European discoveries regarding math and science?

* *Unreality:* Do the materials, for example, gloss over unpleasant facts and events in history, such as the degree to which a genocide was committed against Native Americans?

* *Fragmentation and Isolation:* Do the materials, for example, present information in a fragmented way, such as providing an isolated box separate from the main textual materials entitled "Ten Black Achievers in Science"?

* *Linguistic Bias:* Do the materials, for example, describe non-English speakers as "alien"?

* *Cosmetic Bias:* Do the materials, for example, suggest that the materials are bias free by displaying a cover that is multicultural, even though the narrative in the text is exclusionary?

• *Promote multicultural education.* Examine your school or district through a multicultural lens. Multicultural education consists of five dimensions: content integration (e.g., the degree to which teachers use examples from a variety of cultures), equity pedagogy (e.g., teaching that facilitates achievement for all students), empowering school culture and structure (e.g., practices that avoid labeling), prejudice reduction (e.g., activities that promote positive interactions with those different from oneself), and knowledge construction (e.g., examining who determines what gets taught) (Banks, 1997).

Reflective Question

1. Assess your personal degree of impartiality. In what instances were you impartial, or less so?

3. DEMONSTRATING EMPATHY

What does it mean to be an empathetic leader? The word *empathy* conjures up images of individuals, usually female, consoling others in times of crisis or listening carefully to another's story of suffering. What do caring, compassion, and empathy have to do with educational leadership? Why does a principal have to personify empathy to be considered a good leader?

Our image of an administrator has been culturally ingrained as a bureaucrat and autocrat. Although not all of them act as such, autocracy in school administration and supervision has been reinforced by the establishment and maintenance of bureaucratic school governance (Glanz, 1991). Expectations are established for administrators to, first and foremost, maintain organizational stability and adhere to bureaucratic mandates. Authority to carry out their mandates is conferred through hierarchical status. In short, the organization, not the individual, is of paramount importance to such a school administrator.

Framing school leadership on a radically different paradigm of "leadership as ethic of caring" (Noddings, 1984, 1992) is a more useful and potentially empowering conception of school administration. Such a conception supports the notion that our task as principals, for example, is essentially to support and encourage teachers while nurturing children by teaching them to be caring, moral, and productive members of society. As Noddings (1992) explains: "The traditional organization of schooling is intellectually and morally inadequate for contemporary society" (p. 173). Nurturing an "ethic of caring," principals, like teachers, realize that their ultimate motive is to inspire a sense of caring, sensitivity, appreciation, and respect for the human dignity of all people, despite the travails that pervade our society and world. Noddings (1992) makes the point, "We should educate all our children not only for competence but also for caring. Our aim should be to encourage the growth of competent, caring, loving, and lovable people" (p. xiv).

> "Do what you can to show you care about other people, and you will make our world a better place."
>
> —Rosalyn Carter

Feminist organizational theory (Regan, 1990) informs this "ethic of caring" by avoiding traditional conceptions of leadership. Feminist theory questions the legitimacy of the hierarchical, patriarchal, bureaucratic school organization. Challenging traditional leadership models, feminist theory encourages community building, interpersonal relationships, nurturing, and collaboration as of primary interest. Although much literature in the field suggests that women as educational leaders are more attuned to fostering intimate relationships that accentuate an ethic of caring, it seems reasonable to think that persons of both genders are just as likely to demonstrate that they are concerned with teaching, learning, instruction, curriculum, and people. Some argue that because women "spend more time as teachers and as mothers before they become administrators; they produce more positive interactions with community and staff; they have a more democratic, inclusive, and conflict-reducing style; and they are less concerned with bureaucracy" (Marshall, 1995, p. 488). The difference does not lie inherently in gender. Women can exhibit some rather officious, domineering behaviors as well as demonstrate autocratic and bureaucratic tendencies. Men, conversely, can be as nurturing and caring as some women. Although women in our society and culture are more easily accepted as sensitive, sympathetic administrators and men less so, both genders have the same capacity for caring and nurturing that are crucial in engendering a spirit and ethic of caring.

Unlike traditional humanistic models of administration, "caring" is inclusive, nonmanipulative, and empowering. Whereas the main objective of bureaucracy is standardization, caring inspires individual responsibility. Starratt (1993) provides support for an ethic of caring in educational administration. According to Starratt (1993), an administrator committed to an ethic of caring will "be grounded in the belief that the integrity of human relationships should be held sacred and that the school as an organization should hold the good of human beings within it as sacred" (p. 195).

How do principals demonstrate caring and empathy? They (a) listen to the other's perspective, (b) respond appropriately to the awareness that comes from this reception, and (c) remain committed to others and to the relationship. Moreover, caring and empathetic principals frequently develop relationships that are the grounds for motivating, cajoling, and inspiring others to excellence. Generally thoughtful and sensitive, they see nuances in people's efforts at good performance and acknowledge them; they recognize the diverse and individual qualities in people and devise individual standards of expectation, incentives, and rewards. (Marshall, Patterson, Rogers, & Steele, 1996, p. 282)

An empathetic principal, therefore, should put people first and policy second. Empathy is integral to the effectiveness of a principal.

Why is empathy such a vital virtue? If you have empathy, you have compassion for others. Caring for others communicates that they are important, worthwhile, and esteemed individuals. Treating people with such compassion will encourage them to respond in kind, to you and to others. Such behavior inspires them to do their utmost to help others. *Empathy*, then, is defined as the extent to which a principal can sense, identify with, and understand what another person is feeling.

As a principal you can best actualize your role as an empathetic leader if you:

• *Demonstrate through your actions that people come first.* I'll never forget the time when I was a teacher and our car pool was stuck in a massive traffic jam on one of the major thoroughfares in the city. The entire office knew about the traffic jam, because the office secretaries always had the radio on in the office in the morning. We eventually arrived, although 45 minutes late. Although the principal knew the reason we were late, he charged, "How dare you be so unprofessional?" I tried to explain our situation, to no avail. He retorted, "You should have had alternate means of transportation." He abruptly left the room, and we, dismayed and shell-shocked, proceeded to our classrooms. This principal clearly did not empathize with us. According to his view, we should have anticipated the traffic and left home 1 hour earlier, as he had done. Right or wrong, his treatment of us that morning was upsetting, lamentable, and unforgettable. How have you recently demonstrated that people come first?

- *Communicate an "ethic of caring."* Improve your listening skills. The next time a staff member has experienced a personal challenge, ask her or him about what happened. Listen, say you're sorry, and offer to help in any way. That's it; that's all you should or could do. Also, inspire all those you meet to aspire to excellence. Offer them the means to do so by providing appropriate resources and suggestions, if they inquire (Noddings, 1992).

Reflective Question

1. Assess your personal degree of empathy. In what instances were you empathetic, or less so?

---

4. JUDGING ETHICALLY

What does it mean to possess good judgment? The word *judgment* conjures up images of someone in authority rendering decisions in the manner of King Solomon. A good judge is said to possess much knowledge. Yet, the mere accumulation of knowledge will not suffice for becoming truly wise. To paraphrase John Dewey, "Learning is not wisdom; information does not guarantee good judgment." Wisdom is the ability to take that accumulated knowledge and apply it intelligently to a particular situation. Judgment is the ability needed to know how to apply knowledge sensibly.

Using good judgment in making decisions is clearly important to a principal. A principal may indeed act courageously (standing behind one's principles), demonstrate impartiality (a commitment to maintain a nonpartisan position), and exhibit empathy (identifying with another's pain). Yet, without good judgment, a principal is completely ineffective, because one's "good" intentions may be misplaced or, worse, detrimental to the school or district. How does a principal learn good judgment?

Judgment is a special talent that cannot be taught but is rather gained from experience and practice. Possessing sound judgment means that one can make decisions intelligently. Judgment is the ability to consider the weight of various facts and information in order to determine their relevance to a particular situation. Hence, the ability to critically think is integral to good judgment.

Principals are action researchers; they are detectives of sorts. They test the validity of various proposals by developing hypotheses and testing them in the real world. They collect an array of data in order to intelligently make decisions. They are not neutral technicians who merely dictate policies without appropriate follow-up. They possess professional knowledge and technical skills that enable them to analyze and solve problems with insight and imagination.

> "Judgment, a critical element in leadership decision making, has two components. One is knowledge. A leader cannot make a judgment if he is unfamiliar with the subject about which the judgment must be made. . . . The other component is common sense, which is an attribute that individuals attain through experience."
>
> —General Robert H. Barrow

A principal who possesses good judgment, therefore, has the ability to sift through myriad data, select what's relevant, weigh the relevant data against the pressing needs of the moment, and make a decisive decision. A principal who lacks judgment may possess some other virtues, but she or he is destined to fail because good leadership is about making thoughtful, reasoned decisions.

The possession of knowledge does not guarantee that one can succeed in educational leadership or that one will exercise good judgment with respect to work in a particular area. Good judgment in the context of educational leadership requires that the principal have a firm grounding in the educational enterprise (i.e., must be well versed in all areas of education) combined with a keen awareness of the complex factors that impinge on school practice. Good judgment requires knowledge, reflection in and on action, and the ability to consider a wide array of factors, sometimes simultaneously and immediately.

As a principal, you can best actualize your role as a good judge if you:

- *Sharpen your critical-thinking skills.* Anyone who has worked as a principal realizes that "educational leadership is riddled (or blessed) with situations that demand quick action and almost immediate response" (Beck, 1994, p. 128). Donald Schon (1987) describes a type of critical (reflective) thinking called *reflection-in-action,* which is the ability to "think on one's feet" when faced with the many surprises and challenges in our daily lives as principals. Principals who are successful certainly are able to "think on their feet" as they face the multitude of crises that are all too common in a school or district. Because judgment is about taking one's knowledge and applying it intelligently—and in most cases "on the spot"—one cannot easily follow a formula that ensures that the best judgment will be made. Practice is the best teacher, but developing critical-thinking skills can't hurt. Consult many of the fine works that help sharpen your thinking skills; many of them are fun at any age! (see, e.g., Paul, 1993).

• *Engage in reflective practice.* Schon (1987) also discusses a second type of reflective thinking, *reflection-on-action.* Reflection-on-action occurs when educational leaders look back upon their work and consider thoughtfully what practices were successful and what areas need improvement. Too busy? Can't find the time? Try this suggestion, and you'll discover that judgment making can be enhanced: Schedule time on your calendar, during the least hectic time of day (e.g., 1:45–2:00 p.m.), to close your door, take the phone off the hook, and consider one area that requires careful consideration (e.g., "Should I hire that new teacher candidate?").

• *Undertake action research.* Action research is a powerful tool of disciplined inquiry that enables a leader to carefully and systematically reflect on practice. Follow these four easy steps: (a) select a focus of concern, (b) collect data, (c) analyze and interpret the data, and (d) take action (Glanz, 2003).

Reflective Question

1. Assess your personal degree of judgment. In what instances did you use good judgment, or less so?

---

5. REMAINING HUMBLE

What does it mean to be a humble principal? The word *humility* conjures up images of subservience, deference, and meekness, qualities antithetical to a leader. In fact, principals are invested with authority within the educational hierarchy. They have high salaries, a separate union, their own offices, and even private parking spaces. Moreover, they are usually highly credentialed and have special advanced certifications. They are usually more experienced than teachers, who are lower in the hierarchy. How could such leaders exhibit humility? Indeed, why should they?

Many people's understanding of humility is skewed. Many people think that to demonstrate humility indicates low self-esteem. The truth of the matter is that the more confident a principal is, the greater capacity she or he has for humility. Humble principals prefer to stay in the background, but not because they are shy, reticent, or insecure. They are confident and secure enough in their own accomplishments to herald the achievements of others. As one principal put it, "I prefer to act in such a way that my assets are not trumpeted on my sleeve, but rather are known by my actions." Humble principals are not "proud of their humility." The challenge of good principals is to learn how to negotiate the delicate balance between expertise and humility.

Pretentiousness, arrogance, and conceit are anathema to good principals. Good principals do not hold on to dogmatic beliefs about "best practices." No one has a panacea to solve all the school's problems. In contrast, the prototypical autocrat lacks humility and is devoid of reverence for children and their teachers. A humble principal, therefore, acknowledges the tentativeness of his or her suggestions and also respects teaching and teachers.

Humble principals live paradoxically. On the one hand, they realize their strengths, accomplishments, and capabilities; on the other hand, they are cognizant of their limitations. These leaders lack arrogance, are affirming of the abilities of others, and eschew personal accolades. These self-effacing principals are highly respected and beloved in the organization. Rarely will you find much discussion of this important virtue in the literature on leadership. Humility is being aware of one's limitations while at the same time being cognizant of one's abilities.

You can best actualize your role as a humble principal if you:

• *Empower others and give them the credit.* As a confident leader, you feel comfortable in empowering others to participate in school improvement initiatives. You lead by example and are ready, willing, and able to stand in the background to allow others to take the credit. As long as you are attaining your objectives, you are not concerned about receiving all the credit. You realize that a good principal is one who can empower others to share their leadership qualities in order to achieve a "greater good." I am reminded of something that Robert Woodruff of Coca-Cola once said about this important aspect of leadership, "Man [*sic*] can accomplish great success if he doesn't care who gets the credit" (quoted in Blumenthal, 2001, p. 19).

• *Highlight the accomplishments of others.* Identify deserving individuals and find ways to positively reinforce and acknowledge their herculean efforts on behalf of the school or district. Acknowledge them continuously (not just in an end-of-year letter). Humble, secure principals will not hesitate to reward others for a job well done. In my experience, principals often don't do so for a variety of reasons, including personal insecurities ("If I acknowledge John, then they'll think he ran the show"), frustrations ("Well, no one ever acknowledges my accomplishments"), and the belief that people don't deserve rewards ("After all, that's why he's getting paid"). Humble principals realize the importance of highlighting the accomplishments of others.

Reflective Question

1. Assess your personal degree of humility. In what instances were you humble, or less so?

CONCLUSION

Schools will not renew themselves with principals who are cowards, biased, indifferent, poor judges, and arrogant. We need, in contrast, principals who have an awareness of their own ignorance but who at the same time are not afraid to stand behind programs and practices that are controversial; leaders who are committed to treating people (children, parents, and others) fairly and justly; leaders who can appreciate and sense others' hurt and who can weigh complex factors in rendering decisions.

Educators must rethink their goals and refocus their emphases to the enduring and profound qualities we want principals to possess. Beyond technical competence, to paraphrase Hare (1993), do we want principals with a limited sense of their moral, intellectual, and personal qualities? Or should we demand principals who are ethical, empowered, and confident? Do we want principals who are arrogant, dogmatic, and insensitive? Or do we want principals who have humility, courage, and empathy?

The final chapter focuses on helping you address those thorny, practical ethical dilemmas you face on a daily basis.

C H A P T E R F O U R

Approaches to Resolving Ethical Dilemmas

"Leading with moral purpose calls for an examination of your assumptions about what is ethical and what is unethical, how far you are willing to go to advance your core values and do the right thing, what you are willing to risk to achieve the values of justice and fairness, and how you will wrestle with an inconsistency between your values and the values of your organization. The goal is not to discover easy answers or quick fixes to these issues but to engage in an ethical analysis and to use your moral imagination in solving problems and dilemmas."

—Susan Komives, Nance Lucas,
and Timothy McMahon

"When making decisions involving ethical dilemmas, principals exercise moral authority. . . . Yet . . . few principals have been trained to analyze these types of conflicts because ethical issues have been given little attention in preparation programs for administrators."

—David A. Sousa

O ne of the major themes of this work is that resolving ethical dilemmas is no easy task, and there are no ready-made recipes or guidelines to follow. As a critical thinker with a well-thought-out belief system, you will be challenged to think on your feet as you confront situations that require ethical decision making. In this chapter, we will introduce several decision-making models you can apply to any given situation. The models are illustrative, not exhaustive, regarding the approaches that are feasible. Although these three models provide specific factors to keep in mind when making decisions about ethical or moral issues, the following commonsense, but too often overlooked, approach should be kept in mind:

- Identify the dilemma or issue precisely (e.g., organization vs. individual issue).
- Gather as much data as you can from all perspectives (in other words, seek to understand the dilemma or issue in all its complexities). This stage may involve interviewing all parties, reviewing school or district policies, and so forth. At this time, take no action. Seek to understand by gathering data.
- Clarify the issue now that you have gathered the data (in other words, get more specific than the first step).
- Reflect deeply about the issue. Take your time. Seek counsel if possible. Don't rush into a decision. Wait at least 1 full day for deliberation. Think about the consequences of your decision for all concerned parties, including the school climate and culture.
- Make the decision decisively.
- "Live with [the] decision and learn from it" (Maxcy, 2002, p. 154).

What You Should Know About Resolving Ethical Dilemmas

- **The Rest Model**—Principals should exhibit moral sensitivity, moral judgment, moral motivation, and moral action when working through an ethical dilemma.
- **Five Principles of Ethics**—Principals must respect autonomy, do no harm, benefit others, be just, and be faithful when undertaking ethical decision making.
- **Twelve Questions**—Principals should pose 12 questions before making any ethical decision.

1. UTILIZING THE REST MODEL

Komives and colleagues (1998) relate James Rest's (1986) practical decision-making model, which provides four stages of a model based on "moral reasoning and an ethic of care" (p. 265). This discussion is also informed by a study recently conducted by Klinker and Hackmann (2004). The Rest Model attempts to help us understand and predict moral behavior and decision making. According to Rest, a student of Lawrence Kohlberg, we go through four stages or components when making a decision about an ethical dilemma: sensitivity, judgment, motivation, and courage. If we fail in any one component, then we may make a poor decision.

Rest's Four-Component Decision-Making Model, drawn from Komives and colleagues (1998, p. 266), is outlined below:

Component I: Moral Sensitivity (interpreting the situation as moral)

  A. Being aware of the situation's moral dimension, that is, that the welfare of another person is at stake
  B. Recognizing how possible courses of action affect all parties involved

Component II: Moral Judgment (defining the morally ideal course of action)

  A. Determining what should be done
  B. Formulating a plan of action that applies a moral standard or ideal (e.g., justice)

Component III: Moral Motivation (deciding what to do)

  A. Evaluating the various courses of action for how they would serve moral or nonmoral values (e.g., political sensitivity, professional aspirations)
  B. Deciding what to do

Component IV: Moral Action (executing and implementing a moral plan of action)

  A. Acting as one intended to act; following through with that decision

B. Being assisted by perseverance, resoluteness, strong character, core values, the strength of one's convictions, and so on

Let's say you, as principal, were confronted by the following moral dilemma. You are buddies, personally and socially, with the football coach. His son, who also attends the school, is caught cheating by his 12th-grade history teacher. School policy and precedent demand that the student be brought before the school's Honesty Committee. The football coach pleads with you not to send him before the committee, because a negative finding would jeopardize his son's scholarship to a prestigious university in the Midwest. You have previously reported other students to this committee for similar infractions. Only you and the teacher know about the incident. What would you do?

Using Component I of the Rest Model, you realize that this is indeed a moral issue and not something you can simply "push under the rug." You understand the nature of the violation and that other students have been sent before the committee for similar incidents. You also realize that your decision will affect the teacher who reported the incident to you. Should you use your authority over this untenured teacher to quell the matter? What impact will your decision have on this teacher? Is it fair to place the teacher in such a situation?

Under Component II, you pause and consider the morally ideal situation. What would you do if you were not friendly with the boy's father? What have you done in the past? Consider the matter of justice and equity, that is, treating all students fairly in similar situations. Now, under Component III, you have to decide what to do. Consider what impact your decision will have on the participants, the school, and the community at large. What impact will your decision have on the ethical climate of your school? What message will you be sending if the matter becomes public knowledge? In Component IV, consider what you would do if it became public knowledge that you allowed the student to "slide" in this case. How will this decision affect future decisions? Was the decision the morally proper thing to do? Explain why or why not.

Klinker and Hackmann (2004) conducted a study of 104 secondary administrators who received State Principal of the Year awards. Respondents completed a questionnaire that included narratives reflecting scenarios likely to be encountered by principals, including student discipline and teacher evaluation issues. Respondents were asked to make action choices and provide justifications to resolve the dilemmas. Klinker and Hackmann's research questions were: (1) Do principals make ethical decisions in accordance with an ethical standard? and (2) What justifications do the respondents use for making ethical decisions? Quantitative and qualitative data analyses were undertaken.

Four themes emerged from the study: courage, the common good, gut feelings, and difficulty in defining ethics. Principals reported that making tough ethical decisions took a lot of courage (see discussion of courage in Chapter 3). Principals made decisions, Klinker and Hackmann (2004) reported, based on benefit for everyone or the common good. For instance, one principal stated that although he felt bad about having to terminate a teacher with only 4 years left to retirement, he made his decision based on what he felt was best for the school. Very significantly, principals explained that decision making involved investigating the case thoroughly, remaining aware and sensitive to others' needs, listening for different points of view, and examining all aspects of the problem. Yet, when it came down to making a decision, these top principal leaders used their "gut" feelings. As one respondent put it, "It's a gut feeling. An emotion, I can't explain it" (Klinker & Hackmann, 2004, p. 449). Finally, principals reported that although they made ethical choices, they had a hard time defining *ethics.*

Results of the study indicated that although a majority of these principals were able to select the most appropriate action response to a case situation, at least one third "selected inappropriate actions for two of the three narratives." "Moreover," Klinker and Hackmann (2004) continue, "respondents had difficulty understanding the processes through which they made their decisions" (p. 453).

The authors concluded that when confronted with ethical dilemmas, principals must fully examine their own beliefs and values and try to base their judgments in rational processes. They conclude, "Ethical decisions are nested within social, emotional, and psychological contexts. Understanding this complexity of contexts can be helpful to beginning administrators and assist them in making appropriate ethical decisions" (Klinker & Hackmann, 2004, p. 453).

Reflective Questions

1. What's your reaction to the Rest Model? Describe how it may be useful.

2. React to the Klinker and Hackmann (2004) study. What did you learn that was surprising?

3. The authors of the aforementioned study explained that principals should be encouraged to practice self-reflection and self-awareness of the biases and values that we bring to the job. How does reflection assist us in making better decisions?

4. What do the authors mean by the following statement: "Blasted by demands and buffeted by competing values, the good principal can make a bad decision unless grounded in her or his own ethical filters of courage, motivation, judgment, and sensitivity" (Klinker & Hackmann, 2004, p. 453)?

---

2. ATTENDING TO THE FIVE PRINCIPLES OF ETHICS

Komives and colleagues (1998) also explain the five principles of ethics highlighted by Beauchamp and Childress (1979): (a) respecting autonomy, (b) doing no harm, (c) benefiting others, (d) being just, and (e) being faithful. As principal, you can "use these five principles as a critical evaluative approach to moral reasoning and ethical decision-making" (Komives et al., p. 267).

Five Ethical Principles in Decision Making

(drawn from Komives et al., 1998, p. 268)

1. *Respecting autonomy* means providing leaders and members with the freedom of choice, allowing individuals to freely develop their values, and respecting the right of others to act independently. Autonomy, like constitutional rights and liberties,

has conditions and does not imply unrestricted freedom. A major assumption of autonomy is that an individual possesses a certain level of competence to make rational and informed decisions.

2. *Doing no harm (nonmaleficence)* involves providing an environment that is free from harm to others, both psychological and physical. Leaders refrain from actions that can harm others.

3. *Benefiting others (beneficence)* means promoting the interests of the organization above personal interests and self-gain. The notion of promoting what is good for the whole of the organization or community and promoting the growth of the group is upheld in the principle of beneficence.

4. *Being just (justice)* refers to treating people fairly and equally. This principle is traced to Aristotle's work on ethics.

5. *Being faithful (fidelity)* involves keeping promises, being faithful, and being loyal to the group or organization. Being faithful is a principle premised on relationships and trust. If you as a leader or member violate the principle of fidelity, it is difficult or impossible for others to develop a trusting relationship.

Komives and colleagues (1998) provide a scenario that can relate to your role as principal. You are in charge of the multicultural fair at your school. A subcommittee designs a T-shirt that you find offensive, in that it may offend certain ethnic groups. The subcommittee spent $5,000 on the shirts. Some teachers complain about the message conveyed by the logo. Komives and colleagues ask:

> Which of the five principles would you use in working through this dilemma? Do any of the principles clash with one another, such as respecting the autonomy of the committee and doing no harm to those who might be hurt by the symbolism on the T-shirt? (p. 269)

Reflective Question

1. Can you think of a scenario in which you might apply the five ethical principles? Explain in detail.

3. RAISING 12 QUESTIONS WHEN MAKING A DECISION

Komives and colleagues (1998, p. 270) cite Nash (1987), who presents another model for addressing ethical dilemmas. He poses 12 questions to ask yourself before you make a decision or take any action related to the ethical problem at hand.

1. Have you defined the problem accurately?

2. How would you define the problem if you stood on the other side of the fence?

3. How did this situation occur in the first place?

4. To whom and to what do you give your loyalty as a person and as a member of the organization?

5. What is your intention in making this decision?

6. How does this intention compare with the probable results?

7. Whom could your decision or action injure?

8. Can you discuss the problem with the affected parties before you make your decision?

9. Are you confident that your position will be as valid over a long period of time as it seems now?

10. Could you disclose without qualms your decision or action to your boss, the president of the board of directors, your family, or society as a whole?

11. What is the symbolic potential of your action if understood? If misunderstood?

12. Under what conditions would you allow exceptions to your stand?

It comes to your attention that Mr. Hamilton shoved Shaheim, one of the class's most difficult students, out of frustration. Shaheim fell into the stairwell banister and now complains of shoulder pain. No other student or faculty member witnessed the incident. It's Shaheim's word against the teacher's word.

Mr. Hamilton privately admits the indiscretion to you. Mr. Hamilton is one of your best teachers, always willing to take the more difficult students in the school. Shaheim's mother is coming up to see you about the incident. Mr. Hamilton asks you to back his version of the story. Work through each of Nash's 12 questions to help clarify a possible course of action.

Reflective Question

1. How do the 12 questions in total or individually help in resolving ethical dilemmas you may encounter?

CONCLUSION

These ethical decision-making models can help you reach a more informed and carefully analyzed decision before you take any action. Too often, we are tempted to quickly put out fires or react to pressing dilemmas without engaging in a process that would provide some assurance that the right decision was made. These models alone will not necessarily help you resolve every dilemma you encounter. They provide a framework to guide your decision making, but they do not provide the moral imagination and creative thinking that are needed to address complex situations. That is up to you.

Conclusion

The Moral Imperatives of School Leadership

"The moral purpose of educators may seem universal, but it has too often emerged as an individual phenomenon—the heroic teacher, principal, or superintendent who succeeds for brief periods against all odds. This moral martyrdom is great for the individual's soul, but it does not lead to sustainable reform. We need, instead, to think of the moral imperative as an organizational or systemic quality."

—Michael Fullan, Al Bertani, and Joanne Quinn

"In a high-stakes context, school leaders must search for ways to create a culture of high expectations and support for all students and a set of norms around teacher growth that enables teachers to teach all students well."

—Linda Lambert

"It is time we had a new kind of accountability in education—one that gets back to the moral basics of caring, serving, empowering and learning."

—Michael Fullan and Andy Hargreaves

"The essential value of the public school in a democracy . . . [is] to ensure an educated citizenry capable of participating

in all discussions, debates, and decisions to further the well-ness of the larger community and protect the individual right to 'life, liberty, and the pursuit of happiness.'"

—Carl D. Glickman

"Democratic schools in postmodern times require stronger leadership than traditional, top down, autocratic institu-tions. The nature of that leadership, however, is markedly different, replacing the need to control with the desire to support. Ironically, such leaders exercise much more influ-ence where it counts, creating dynamic relationships between teachers and students in the classroom and result-ing in high standards of academic achievement."

—Eric Nadelstern, Janet R. Price, and Aaron Listhaus

Stated succinctly, precisely, and forthrightly, a major moral imperative of leadership revolves around the primacy of high expectations and achievement for all students. Ultimately, we will and should be judged by the degree to which we have contributed to quality instruction that promotes high achievement for all our children. Effective leadership must be inti-mately connected to promoting student achievement.

As identified by Waters, Marzano, and McNulty (2004), research indicates that leadership has been highly correlated with these critical areas of leadership:

- *Culture:* fosters shared beliefs and a sense of community and cooperation
- *Order:* establishes a set of standard operating procedures and routines
- *Discipline:* protects teachers from issues and influences that would detract from their teaching time or focus
- *Resources:* provides teachers with the materials and profes-sional development necessary for the successful execution of their jobs

- *Curriculum, instruction, and assessment:* is directly involved in the design and implementation of curriculum, instruction, and assessment practices
- *Knowledge of curriculum, instruction, and assessment:* is knowledgeable about current practices
- *Focus:* establishes clear goals and keeps these goals at the forefront of the school's attention
- *Visibility:* has high-quality contact and interactions with teachers and students
- *Contingent rewards:* recognizes and rewards individual accomplishments
- *Communication:* establishes strong lines of communication with teachers and students
- *Outreach:* is an advocate and spokesperson for the school to all stakeholders
- *Input:* involves teachers in the design and implementation of important decisions and policies
- *Affirmation:* recognizes and celebrates school accomplishments and acknowledges failures
- *Relationship:* demonstrates empathy with teachers and staff on a personal level
- *Change agent role:* is willing and prepared to actively challenge the status quo
- *Optimizer role:* inspires and leads new and challenging innovations
- *Ideals and beliefs:* communicates and operates from strong ideals and beliefs about schooling
- *Monitoring and evaluation:* monitors the effectiveness of school practices and their impact on student learning
- *Flexibility:* adapts his or her leadership behavior to the needs of the current situation and is comfortable with dissent
- *Situational awareness:* is aware of the details and undercurrents in the running of the school and uses this information to address current and potential problems
- *Intellectual stimulation:* ensures that faculty and staff are aware of the most current theories and practices in education and makes the discussion of these practices integral to the school's culture (Waters et al., 2004, pp. 49–50)

Principals, then, should be involved in these leadership areas. However, although promoting student achievement is primary, it is by no means our sole moral imperative. Hence, the word *imperatives*, connoting the plural, appears in the title of this Conclusion. Allow me to share some thoughts about these "moral imperatives." Although they may appear a bit random, or arbitrary, if you will, and other educators may choose to highlight others, I think they are nonetheless imperative to maintaining an ethical and spiritual commitment to our work. (Portions of the text below are drawn from my department's conceptual framework, which I authored.)

The events of September 11, 2001, have dramatically altered our view of the world and our conception of education (Apple, 2002). In the months afterward, we emerged, for the most part, with a renewed conviction of the powerful influence of education toward achieving a just, democratic society. Education alone may not put an end to hatred, terror, and atrocities, but it can raise the consciousness of individuals in terms of what it means "to be a caring and just human being in a world rife with indifference, injustice, and brutality" (Totten & Feinberg, 2001, p. 5).

Rawls (1971) has developed a framework for examining justice as a system that is concerned with fairness and equitable treatment for all people. Rawls maintains that justice is contingent on treating all members of society equally. Principals, as effective and caring educators, should be viewed as champions of justice, equality, and opportunity. Principals, like teachers, are committed to the belief that all children, at different rates, can reach their potential. Effective educators value diversity, democracy, and justice. Principals treat everyone with dignity and respect. Guarantees of equal access and equal competence are basic rights of all people (Spring, 1994).

Guided by the overarching goals of equity and social justice (Rapp, 2002; Rawls, 1971), effective leading is, I think, inherently moral work that is guided by an ethic of caring (Hansen, 2001; Jordan Irvine, 2001; Richert, 1998). Framing educational practice as an "ethic of caring" (Noddings, 1984, 1992) is a powerful paradigm to guide our work. Such a paradigm or conception supports the notion that our task as educators is essentially to support, encourage, and nurture children by teaching them to be caring, moral, and productive members of society. As spiritual leaders, we can see the latent potential in each person, even when others might not. We encourage, challenge, and maintain high but reasonable expectations for performance, socially and academically. We care enough about people to envision possibilities where they or others might not. Before the 4-minute mile record was broken, common knowledge held that it was impossible. Yet when Roger Benniser broke it, within a year the record was again broken by others. He showed the way. It no longer provided a mental barrier for people. So, too, we show the way to others through a leadership of caring and justice for all people in our school. That work is inherently essential and spiritual.

Pedagogical practice that is thoughtful, deliberate, and critical is very much consonant with an educational practice based on an ethic of caring (Barone, 2001; Kate, Noddings, & Strike, 1999; Steinberg, 1995; Villa & Thousand, 2000; Wink, 2000). Principals guide teachers to demonstrate their concern for students through reflective work that requires active and systematic inquiry (LaBoskey & Cline, 2000; Loughran, 2002). Principals encourage teachers to motivate students to construct meaning on their own. Constructivism is not a theory about teaching and learning per se; rather, it is a theory about the nature of knowledge itself. Knowledge is seen as temporary, developmental, socially constructed, culturally mediated, and nonobjective. Learning, then, becomes a self-regulated process wherein the individual resolves cognitive conflicts while engaged in concrete experiences, intellectual discourse, and critical reflection (Foote, Vermette, & Battaglia, 2001; Rodgers, 2002). Kolb's (1984) experiential learning model is indicative of such a constructivist approach.

Although critical pedagogy involves constructivist theory and practice, it also, and perhaps more significantly, underscores participative democracy (inclusionary practices) and personifies a pedagogy of hope. Young (2000), in *Inclusion and Democracy*, argues that the pursuit of democracy enhances a "just society" fostering social change. Martin (2001) states that democratic and equitable constructivist teaching and learning should command center stage in education.

Inclusion is a belief system. It is a process of facilitating an educational environment that provides access to high-quality education for all students (e.g., McLeskey & Waldron, 2001;

Wolfendale, 2000). Effective principals believe that all children learning together in the same schools and the same classrooms, with services and supports necessary so that they can succeed, is critical. Maintaining high expectations for all students, believing in their potential, and providing needed services for full participation are essential. Children should not be demeaned or have their uniqueness ignored or belittled. Students with disabilities should be educated with students without disabilities as much as possible. Special classes or removal of children from the regular education environment should occur only when the nature or severity of the disability is such that education in the regular classroom cannot be achieved satisfactorily, even with the use of supplementary support services (Elliott & McKenney, 1998; Morse, 2002).

Practices that are inclusionary are based on democratic thought and are a hope for the future. Such hopeful thinking is reflected in the writings of Clough and Corbet (2000); Freire (1974, 1994); Kohl (1998); Macedo (1994); McLaren (2000); and Oakes and Lipton (1999).

Paulo Freire (1974) was correct when he said that if we want students to go out and make a difference in the world, then they have to feel able to make a change in the world around them. One key component in this process is a problem-finding, problem-posing education. Students not only need to be in the habit of solving other people's problems (e.g., those of teachers and other authorities), that is, a "problem-solving education," but they also need to be able to find the problems that they think need to be solved. A moral imperative, then, is to serve as a transformational leader. To problem-solve and serve as a change agent and to encourage others to do so is part of transformational leadership. As a transformational leader, you are deeply involved in making a difference through your work.

The moral imperatives of leadership, then, involve much work as you strive to enhance student achievement, to work for democracy, to believe in the power of education to transform, to herald caring and justice, to engage in reflective practice, to model constructivist work, to promote inclusive practice, and to serve as a transformational leader. To accomplish these moral imperatives requires commitment, strength, and spirit.

Spiritual leadership underlies these moral imperatives. Without a commitment or understanding of the spirit, you work strictly on a perfunctory level. You may work to promote democracy or inclusive practices, for example, but without a deep appreciation that your work is spiritual, you are likely to falter when the going gets tough. Spiritual leadership means that you are driven to accomplish your goals because they are fundamental to your beliefs and values. You are a person of conviction, deeply grounded and resolute. You rely on an inner strength and a vast vision to ensure that your goals are met. According to Thompson (2004), "Developing a spiritual approach to education leadership . . . can be the anchor that helps leaders stay grounded and tightly focused on the high goal of improving education for all students" (p. 63).

Resource A

Realities of Ethical and Spiritual Leadership: In-Basket Simulations

T his section highlights some of the realities of ethical and spiritual leadership using an approach called "In-Basket Simulations." It is a study technique derived from an approach used when I studied for licensure as a principal in New York City. The approach was developed by the Institute for Research and Professional Development (http://www.nycenet .edu/opm/opm/profservices/rfp1b723.html). Scenarios that you might encounter as a principal are presented for your reaction. For instance, "A letter from an irate parent complaining that her child is intentionally being ignored during instruction in class by the teacher is sent to your attention. What would you do?" Challenging you to confront real-life phenomena under controlled conditions, these simulated in-basket items will prompt critical inquiry. Also, as you respond to these short scenarios, ask yourself, "What is the underlying moral or ethical issue?"

Here are suggestions to guide you as you complete these in-basket exercises:

1. Think and respond as if you are a principal, not a teacher or an assistant principal.

2. Place yourself mentally in each situation as if the case were actually happening to you.

3. Draw on your experiences and from what you've learned from others. Think of a principal you respect, and ask yourself, "What would Mr. or Ms. X have done?"

4. Make distinctions between actions you would personally take and actions you would delegate to others.

5. Utilize resources (personnel or otherwise) to assist you.

6. Think about your response, and then share it with a colleague for reaction.

7. Record your response, and then a day later reread the scenario and your response. Would you still have reacted the same way?

Please note that other books provide longer case studies that serve as an excellent way of reflecting on moral dilemmas. Refer to Maxcy (2002), Strike and colleagues (2005), and Zubay and Soltis (2005).

During an interview, you are asked to respond to the following scenarios:

• You are confronted by an irate parent who claims that a well-respected teacher hit her child after school in the school yard. The parent demands that the teacher be fired and refuses to leave your office until the teacher is brought down to speak with her.

• You receive a call from a teacher 10 minutes before dismissal; she tells you that she intends to frisk all her students and not let them leave because her purse is missing.

• Teachers listen to you talk about the "soul" of teaching. A few teachers approach you afterward to complain that they don't appreciate your raising religious issues during a faculty meeting.

• You see one of your secretaries subtly taking cash from the school lunch jar and placing it in her pocket. You confront her privately, and although she initially denies the accusation, she later admits the offense. She pleads with you to give her a chance and not report or fire her because she's had a stellar 2 years at the school.

• A teacher breaks the copyright law by distributing handouts to students without gaining permission from the publisher.

• A student is caught plagiarizing and is brought to your office by the teacher. The teacher is vehement in his insistence that the girl be made an example of and expelled from the school.

• A teacher has his 12th-grade students develop a campaign to elect one of the local politicians who is currently running for reelection. The teacher obviously favors the candidate and solicits student help with the campaign after school.

• The influential school board president asks you to hire his nephew for a teaching position, although he may not be the best candidate.

• A teacher reports to you that Maria, a ninth grader, seems "depressed."

• The coach approaches you to let his star football player play in Saturday's game despite a very low grade point average.

• A PTA mom asks you for special preference for her child to enter a special program, even though the child is only minimally competent.

• The superintendent informs you that a teacher called her today to report that you violated a school policy.

• You are committed to social justice. You decide to review teacher applications only from people from underrepresented groups.

• A relative asks you to divulge some private information about a student in your school; in doing so, you'd violate the Buckley Amendment.

• A female teacher confides to you that she has secretly tape-recorded conversations that she has had with your assistant principal; the tapes allegedly demonstrate his sexual harassment of her.

• Someone tells you something in confidence. You agree to listen. The information you hear, however, shocks you. You feel you need to confront the individual mentioned in the communication, because not doing so might negatively affect a committee's work.

• You personally dislike Fred Stevens, a seventh-grade teacher. You can't explain why. Later in the month, you need to send a teacher to a local conference to represent the grade. You can send Sam Blanchard, but he doesn't have the skills necessary. Fred would be an ideal choice. You hesitate to select Fred because of your feelings toward him.

- Mr. Hal McCullough, principal of Jones Intermediate School, obtains grant money from the district office for the multi-cultural fair. Although grant regulations indicate that he doesn't have discretion to use the funds for projects other than the fair, he decides to use some money to fund the literacy program.

- You discover that your assistant principal has been making numerous personal calls from the school phone in his office to his brother in California. Fifteen calls per month are documented on the school's phone bills. School policy does not permit teachers to make long-distance phone calls from school phones without express permission from you.

- The custodian reports that noxious fumes from exhaust pipes in the school's storage room have filled the lowest floor of the building, a floor usually unoccupied by anyone but custodial workers. He reports that he has called the Department of Safety, which is sending over two officials to inspect the situation. The custodian tells you he has things under control.

- You're working late one night with no one around. In the serene setting of your office, when the hustle and bustle of the day's activities have waned, you sit back in your chair and take a deep breath. You think about your role as principal and all you want to accomplish. Before you know it, an hour has passed. You slowly rise from your seat with renewed conviction and a plethora of ideas in mind. You can't wait for the next school day to begin. You get to school the next morning and are confronted by the custodian reporting a flood in the basement, a fax from the district office indicating that you are losing your only guidance counselor and an ESL teacher because of budget cuts, and a call from a local reporter requesting your reaction to a story that will run in tomorrow's edition indicating that your school's scores on last year's standardized math test declined by 5%.

Resource B

Assessing Your Role as an
Ethical and Spiritual Leader

As the principal, you realize that your position is fraught with challenges that test your morals and sense of ethics. You also realize that your work is what Gary Zukav (2000) calls "sacred work." You understand the connection between your sense of spirituality and ethical behavior. You realize that you serve as a role model for others in your organization. You also realize that the way you approach your work is critical for enhancing positive school culture and climate. Please complete this questionnaire as a means of self-reflection or analysis in order to assess the extent to which you meet these ethical or spiritual ideals. You realize, of course, that the survey is not scientific, and results therefore should not be studied in that light. Please note that your responses are private. Your honest responses to the various items below will best serve as reflective tools to assist you in becoming an even better ethical and spiritual leader.

SA = Strongly Agree ("For the most part, yes.")
A = Agree ("Yes, but . . .")
D = Disagree ("No, but . . .")
SD = Strongly Disagree ("For the most part, no.")

SA   A   D   SD   1. When confronted with a moral dilemma, I avoid addressing the issue, hoping, at times, that it will go away.

SA   A   D   SD   2. Although I may adhere to some formal Code of Ethics, I realize that good decision-making ability is a complex process of matching personal values with contextual factors.

SA   A   D   SD   3. I am deeply moral, and others who work with me would attest this as well.

SA   A   D   SD   4. Many people are keenly aware that I am a spiritual person.

SA   A   D   SD   5. I intentionally serve as an ethical role model for others.

SA   A   D   SD   6. When confronted with a difficult situation, people know they can rely on me to inspire them or help them resolve the problem or issue.

SA   A   D   SD   7. I am generally contemplative or introspective, and people see me as such.

SA   A   D   SD   8. Most others would say that I try to champion justice and opportunity for all people regardless of race, gender, sexual preference, and so on.

SA   A   D   SD   9. I work very closely with people, because I can easily empathize with their plight or situation.

SA   A   D   SD   10. My superiors would describe me as a person of integrity.

SA   A   D   SD   11. I cheated at one or two times in my professional life, but I acknowledged my mistakes and have tried to strive for improvement.

SA   A   D   SD   12. I have made mistakes that I regret.

SA   A   D   SD   13. I try to do the right things as well as to do things right.

SA   A   D   SD   14. I seek advice from mentors and superiors.

SA   A   D   SD   15. I sometimes spread false rumors.

SA   A   D   SD   16. Others seek my spiritual advice.

SA   A   D   SD   17. I encourage others to achieve their potential.

SA   A   D   SD   18. I often enjoy serene settings where I can view nature and try to relax.

SA   A   D   SD   19. I find it hard to relax.

SA   A   D   SD   20. The ends justify the means.

SA   A   D   SD   21. I spend a great deal of time in reflection, especially examining my past behavior and decisions made.

SA   A   D   SD   22. I often second-guess myself.

SA   A   D   SD   23. I deeply care about those who work for me.

SA   A   D   SD   24. I am not a very good listener.

SA   A   D   SD   25. I'll sometimes say one thing to one person and something else to another.

SA   A   D   SD   26. My prejudices sometimes interfere with my work.

SA   A   D   SD   27. I actively work to combat injustices such as racism.

SA   A   D   SD   28. Others consider me fair and just.

SA   A   D   SD   29. I can sense pain in others.

SA   A   D   SD   30. I "read" people very well.

SA   A   D   SD   31. We have a moral obligation to pay our taxes.

SA   A   D   SD   32. I would not hire an otherwise competent transgendered individual as a teacher in my school.

SA   A   D   SD   33. A group of parents complain about an ad campaign posted by students in favor of gays and lesbians "coming out of the closet." The parents find the ads offensive and demand that you take them down. After some thought, you'd comply with the parents' request.

SA   A   D   SD   34. You need to hire a new social studies teacher. You promise the job to a close friend of a friend. Later, you find a better candidate for the job. You'd make up some excuse to the first candidate in order to hire the better teacher.

SA   A   D   SD   35. I believe in doing whatever brings the greater good to the greatest number.

SA   A   D   SD   36. You are running low on money for the month. You notice that the grocer under-charged you. You'd keep quiet.

SA   A   D   SD   37. You enjoy listening to and relating ethnic jokes.

SA   A   D   SD   38. Almost anyone can justify their actions.

SA   A   D   SD   39. As long as others do not harm me, I don't care what they do.

SA   A   D   SD   40. One of your tenured teachers has recently demonstrated to you that she is burned out. Although a satisfactory teacher in the past, she is now a detriment to her students, academically. You have tried to offer her assistance in many ways, including writing formal letters to her about her behavior. As a tenured teacher, she ignores your attempts to assist her. You know how difficult it is to remove a tenured teacher in your district. You are inundated with so many other matters. Consequently, you'd throw your hands up and give up on the matter.

SA   A   D   SD   41. I often comply with requests when pressured by peers.

SA   A   D   SD   42. I rely on my moral intuition.

SA   A   D   SD   43. A secretary reports that Mr. Smith "eyes" the 11th- and 12th-grade girls. You, too, notice that he's a "looker." Although no student has ever complained about his behavior, you would decide to speak with him about the matter in private.

SA   A   D   SD   44. You would break a school district policy in order to do a favor for a colleague. You know that no one would ever find out, and the matter doesn't involve a very serious issue, although it does involve breaking with stated policy.

SA   A   D   SD   45. I don't get much of a chance for reflection, because my day—and my life—is fraught with challenges and difficulties.

SA   A   D   SD   46. Most other people who work with me would attest that I have a strong sense of right and wrong.

SA   A   D   SD   47. Most other people who work with me
would attest that I am committed to
social justice.

SA   A   D   SD   48. My work as principal is as much spiritual
as it is intellectual and moral.

SA   A   D   SD   49. My personal, cultural values dictate that
loyalty to my family supersedes all else.
Yet, when my cousin asks for a favor that
violates district policy, I have a moral
obligation as principal to enforce
organizational policies over personal
or cultural norms.

SA   A   D   SD   50. Although I am committed to diversity,
I would never hire an unqualified African
American over a white male.

Analyze your responses:

The "answers" below are only suggestive, because no survey can accurately assess your ethical behavior and sense of spirituality. However, the responses below can serve as a basis of comparison and as a means of reflection by yourself or with a colleague.

If you responded Strongly Agree or Agree to these items, then you are

Spiritually sensitive	**A good ethical decision maker**
4, 6, 7, 8, 9, 12, 16, 17, 18, 21, 23, 27, 28, 29, 30, 31, 43, 47, 48	2, 3, 5, 6, 8, 10, 11, 13, 14, 21, 28, 31, 38, 43, 46, 47, 48, 49, 50

If you responded Strongly Disagree or Disagree to these items, then you are

Spiritually sensitive	**A good ethical decision maker**
15, 19, 20, 24, 25, 26, 36, 37, 39, 45	1, 15, 22, 26, 32, 33, 36, 37, 40, 41, 45

Note that items 34, 35, 42, and 44 are much more difficult to categorize.

Reflective Questions

1. How might you use the survey and the explanations to assess your personal sense of spirituality and ethics?

2. What insights into spirituality and ethics have you gained from this exercise?

3. Examine each category and corresponding statement, and explain how you intend to actively change your behavior in order to best promote a sense of spirituality and better ethical decision making.

Resource C

An Annotated Bibliography of Best Resources

The literature on the principalship and related areas is extensive. The list below is not meant to serve as a comprehensive resource by any means. The selected titles I have annotated are few, but, in my opinion, they are among the most useful references on the subject. Rather than "impress" you with a more extensive list, I have selected these outstanding works related specifically to ethical and spiritual leadership that will supplement this book quite well. I may have missed, of course, other important works. Nevertheless, the list below is a good start. Don't forget that life is a long journey of continuous learning. Continue to hone your skills by reading good books and journal articles on ethical and spiritual leadership. No one is ever perfect, and everyone can learn something new by keeping current with the literature in the field. Share your readings and reactions with a colleague.

Ethical Leadership

Maxcy, S. J. (2002). *Ethical school leadership.* Lanham, MD: Scarecrow Press.

   Best resource on the topic; combines theory with practical case study applications.

Strike, K. A., Haller, E. J., & Soltis, J. F. (2005). *The ethics of school administration* (3rd ed.). New York: Teachers College Press.

   Deals with basic philosophical questions such as the following: How do ethical questions differ from factual ones? What is moral or ethical decision making like? Is ethical reasoning really possible? Are not our moral values merely matters of personal choices? Are they not relative to our culture? Can there be objective answers to ethical questions?

Zubay, B., & Soltis, J. (2005). *Creating the ethical school: A book of case studies.* New York: Teachers College Press.

Hands-on manual for dealing with realistic, provocative, and ethically challenging issues. A wide variety of ethical dilemmas on topics including racism, plagiarism, free speech, violence, and so on.

Moral Leadership

Coles, R. (2000). *Lives of moral leadership.* New York: Random House.

Creates a portrait of moral leaders and in doing so provides a glimpse into how to lead a moral life as a leader.

Covey, S. R. (1992). *Principle-centered leadership.* New York: Free Press.

Easy-to-read and -use manual; very popular and recommended.

Goodman, J., & Lesnick, H. (2003). *Moral education: A teacher-centered approach.* Boston: Pearson Allyn & Bacon.

Discusses moral dilemmas in the classroom in a practical and easy-to-use format.

Spiritual Leadership

Bolman, L. G., & Deal, T. E. (1995). *Leading with soul: An uncommon journey.* San Francisco: Jossey-Bass.

Thanks to the authors, administrators are no longer reticent to discuss issues related to soul and spirituality; the authors demystify the terms for leaders.

Kessler, R. (2000). *The soul of education: Helping students find connection, compassion, and character at school.* Alexandria, VA: Association for Supervision and Curriculum Development.

Will help you connect better with the lives of teachers and students, whom you ultimately serve.

Klein, E., & Izzo, J. B. (1998). *Awakening corporate soul: Four paths to unleash the power of people at work.* Lion's Bay, British Columbia, Canada: Fairwinds Press.

Although not written for educators, this volume will give you a good idea of how to put spiritual ideas into practice in any leadership situation.

Moxley, R. S. (2000). *Leadership and spirit: Breathing new vitality and quality into individuals and organizations.* San Francisco: Jossey-Bass.

Clear, engaging, and concise. Good read for skeptics.

Palmer, P. (1993). *To know as we are known: Education as a spiritual journey.* San Francisco: HarperCollins.

Undogmatic and practical, this work is philosophical but still speaks to the practitioner.

Purpel, D. E. (1988). *The moral and spiritual crisis in education: A curriculum for justice and compassion.* Westport, CT: Bergin & Garvey.

A bit scholarly, but incisive and a very interesting read.

Zukav, G. (2000). *Soul stories.* New York: Simon & Schuster.

A book not at all directly related to principalship, but an important read nonetheless. Helps connect us to our personality with discussions about soul awareness. We all have extraordinary creative abilities to sense something beyond the mundane. Lots of stories related to themes of cooperation, harmony, trust, justice, humility, and so forth; an inspirational work.

References

Allport, G. (1987). *The nature of prejudice.* Reading, MA: Addison-Wesley.

Apple, M. (2002). Patriotism, pedagogy, and freedom: On the educational meanings of September 11. *Teachers College Record, 104*(8), 1760–1772. Retrieved March 10, 2005, from http://www.tcrecord.org/content.asp?contentid=10939

Banks, J. (1997). *Educating citizens in a multicultural society.* New York: Teachers College Press.

Barone, T. (2001). *Touching eternity: The enduring outcomes of teaching.* New York: Teachers College Press.

Beauchamp, T. L., & Childress, J. F. (1979). *Principles of biomedical ethics.* New York: Oxford University Press.

Beck, L. G. (1994). *Reclaiming educational administration as a caring profession.* New York: Teachers College Press.

Blumenthal, I. (2001, April). Imperatives of leadership. *Executive Excellence Newsletter, 18,* 19.

Bolman, L. G., & Deal, T. E. (1995). *Leading with soul: An uncommon journey.* San Francisco: Jossey-Bass.

Bolman, L. G., & Deal, T. E. (1997). *Reframing organizations: Artistry, choices, and leadership.* San Francisco: Jossey-Bass.

Brock, B. L., & Grady, M. L. (2004). *Launching your first principalship: A guide for beginning principals.* Thousand Oaks, CA: Corwin.

Buber, M. (1965). *Between man and man.* New York: Macmillan.

Clough, P., & Corbet, J. (2000). *Theories of inclusive education.* Thousand Oaks, CA: Sage.

Drake, T. L., & Roe, W. H. (2003). *The principalship* (6th ed.). Upper Saddle River, NJ: Merrill/Prentice Hall.

Drucker, P. F. (1999). *Management challenges for the 21st century.* New York: HarperBusiness.

Elliott, D., & McKenney, M. (1998). Four inclusion models that work. *Teaching Exceptional Children, 29,* 54–58.

Elmore, F. (2000). *Building a new structure for school leadership.* Washington, DC: Albert Shanker Institute.

Fenstermaker, W. C. (1994). Superintendent decision making: The ethical dimension (Doctoral dissertation, Temple University, 1994). *Dissertation Abstracts International, 55*(08A), 2225.

Foote, C. S., Vermette, P. J., & Battaglia, C. F. (2001). *Constructivist strategies: Meeting standards and engaging adolescent minds.* Larchmont, NY: Eye on Education.

Freire, P. (1974). *Pedagogy of the oppressed.* New York: Seabury Press.

Freire, P. (1994). *The pedagogy of hope: Reliving pedagogy of the oppressed.* New York: Continuum.

Gallegos Nava, R. (2001). *Holistic education: Pedagogy of universal love.* Brandon, VT: Foundation for Educational Renewal.

Gilligan, C. (1993). *In a different voice: Psychological theory and women's development.* Cambridge, MA: Harvard University Press.

Glanz, J. (1991). *Bureaucracy and professionalism: The evolution of public school supervision.* Cranbury, NJ: Fairleigh Dickinson University Press.

Glanz, J. (2002). *Finding your leadership style: A guide for educators.* Alexandria, VA: Association for Supervision and Curriculum Development.

Glanz, J. (2003). *Action research: An educational leader's guide to school improvement* (2nd ed.). Norwood, MA: Christopher-Gordon.

Hansen, D. T. (2001). *Exploring the moral heart of teaching: Toward a teacher's creed.* New York: Teachers College Press.

Hare, W. (1993). *What makes a good teacher: Reflections on some characteristics central to the educational enterprise.* London: Althouse Press.

Hopkins, W. E. (1997). *Ethical dimensions of diversity.* Thousand Oaks, CA: Sage.

Hoyle, J. R. (2002). *Leadership and the force of love.* Thousand Oaks, CA: Corwin.

Hume, D. (1983). *An enquiry concerning the principles of morals.* Indianapolis, IN: Hackett.

Jordan Irvine, J. (2001). *Caring, competent teachers in complex classrooms.* Washington, DC: American Association of Colleges for Teacher Education.

Kant, I. (1966). *Ethical philosophy: The metaphysics of morals* (J. W. Ellington, Trans.). Indianapolis, IN: Hackett.

Kate, M., Noddings, N., & Strike, K. A. (Eds.). (1999). *Justice and caring: The search for common ground in education.* New York: Teachers College Press.

Kessler, R. (2000). *The soul of education: Helping students find connection, compassion, and character in school.* Alexandria, VA: Association for Supervision and Curriculum Development.

Klinker, J. F., & Hackmann, D. G. (2004). An analysis of principals' ethical decision making using Rest's four component model of moral behavior. *Journal of School Leadership, 14,* 434–455.

Kohl, H. (1998). *The discipline of hope: Learning from a lifetime of teaching.* New York: Simon & Schuster.

Kohlberg, L. (1971). Stages in moral development as a basis for moral education. In C. M. Beck, B. S. Crittenden, & E. V. Sullivan (Eds.), *Moral education: Interdisciplinary approaches* (pp. 30–41). Toronto, Ontario, Canada: Toronto University Press.

Kolb, D. (1984). *Experiential learning: Experience as the source of learning and development.* Englewood Cliffs, NJ: Prentice Hall.

Komives, S. R., Lucas, N., & McMahon, T. R. (1998). *Exploring leadership.* San Francisco: Jossey-Bass.

LaBoskey, V. K., & Cline, S. (2000). Behind the mirror: Inquiry-based story in teacher education. *Reflective Practice, 1,* 359–375.

Loughran, J. J. (2002). Effective reflective practice: In search of meaning in learning about teaching. *Journal of Teacher Education, 53,* 33–43.

Lucas, N., & Anello, E. (1995, November). *Ethics and leadership.* Paper presented at the Salzburg Leadership Seminar, Salzburg, Austria.

Macedo, D. (Ed.). (1994). *Literacies of power.* Boulder, CO: Westview Press.

Marshall, C. (1995). Imagining leadership. *Educational Administration Quarterly, 31,* 484–492.

Marshall, C., Patterson, J. A., Rogers, D. L., & Steele, J. R. (1996). Caring as career: An alternative perspective for educational administration. *Educational Administration Quarterly, 32,* 271–294.

Martin, R. (2001). *Listening up: Reinventing ourselves as teachers and students.* Westport, CT: Greenwood.

Maxcy, S. J. (2002). *Ethical school leadership.* Lanham, MD: Scarecrow Press.

McLaren, P. (2000). *Che Guevara, Paulo Freire, and the pedagogy of revolution.* New York: Rowman and Littlefield.

McLeskey, J., & Waldron, N. (2001). *Inclusive schools in action: Making differences ordinary.* Alexandria, VA: Association for Supervision and Curriculum Development.

Morse, T. E. (2002). Designing appropriate curriculum for special education students in urban schools. *Education and Urban Schools, 33,* 4–17.

Nash, L. L. (1987, November). 12 questions to ask when making ethical decisions. *Training & Development, 36.*

Nash, L. L. (1990). *Good intentions aside.* Boston: Harvard Business School Press.

Nietzsche, F. (1973). *Beyond good and evil.* London: Penguin.

Noddings, N. (1984). *Caring: A feminist approach to ethics and moral education.* Berkeley: University of California Press.

Noddings, N. (1992). *The challenge to care in schools: An alternative approach to education.* New York: Teachers College Press.

Noddings, N. (2003). *Caring: A feminine approach to ethics and moral education* (2nd ed.). Berkeley: University of California Press.

Oakes, J., & Lipton, M. (1999). *Teaching to change the world.* New York: McGraw-Hill.

Osterman, K. F., & Kottkamp, R. B. (2004). *Reflective practice for educators* (2nd ed.). Thousand Oaks, CA: Corwin.

Paul, R. (1993). *Critical thinking: What every person needs to survive in a rapidly changing world.* Santa Rosa, CA: Foundation for Critical Thinking.

Portin, B. (with Schneider, P., DeArmond, M., & Gundlach, L.). (2003). *Making sense of leading schools: A study of the school principalship.* Retrieved February 19, 2005, from www.crpe.org/pubs/pdf/Making Sense_PortinWeb.pdf

Rachels, J. (1986). *The elements of moral philosophy.* New York: Random House.

Rapp, D. (2002). Social justice and the importance of rebellious, oppositional imaginations. *Journal of School Leadership, 12,* 226–245.

Rawls, J. (1971). *A theory of justice.* London: Oxford University Press.

Regan, H. B. (1990). Not for women only: School administration as a feminist activity. *Teachers College Record, 91,* 565–577.

Rest, J. R. (1986). Moral development in young adults. In R. A. Mines & K. S. Kitchener (Eds.), *Adult cognitive development: Methods and models* (pp. 92–111). New York: Praeger.

Richert, E. (1998, April). *Preparing the moral practitioner.* Paper presented at the annual meeting of the American Educational Research Association, San Diego, CA.

Rodgers, C. (2002). Seeing student learning: Teacher change and the role of reflection. *Harvard Educational Review, 72,* 230–253.

Schon, D. A. (1987). *Educating the reflective practitioner: Toward a new design for thinking and learning in the professional.* San Francisco: Jossey-Bass.

Sergiovanni, T. J. (1992). *Moral leadership: Getting to the heart of school improvement.* San Francisco: Jossey-Bass.

Sousa, D. A. (2003). *The leadership brain: How to lead in today's schools more effectively.* Thousand Oaks, CA: Corwin.

Spring, J. (1994). *Deculturalization and the struggle for equality: A brief history of the education of dominated cultures in the United States.* New York: McGraw-Hill.

Starratt, R. J. (1993). *The drama of leadership.* London: Falmer.

Starratt, R. J. (1996). *Transforming educational administration: Meaning, community, and excellence.* New York: McGraw-Hill.

Starratt, R. J. (2002). *Ethical leadership.* San Francisco: Jossey-Bass.

Starratt, R. J. (2003). A perspective on ethical educational leadership: An ethics of presence. In F. C. Lunenburg & C. S. Carr (Eds.), *Shaping the future: Policy, partnerships and emerging perspectives* (pp. 146–184). Lanham, MD: Scarecrow Education.

Steinberg, S. (1995). *Turning back: The retreat from racial justice in American thought and policy.* Boston: Beacon Press.

Strike, K., & Soltis, J. F. (1998). *The ethics of teaching.* New York: Teachers College Press.

Strike, K. A., Haller, E. J., & Soltis, J. F. (2005). *The ethics of school adminis-tration* (3rd ed.). New York: Teachers College Press.

Thompson, S. (2004). Leading from the eye of the storm. *Educational Leadership, 61*(7), 60–63.

Totten, S., & Feinberg, S. (2001). *Teaching and studying the Holocaust.* Boston: Allyn & Bacon.

Villa, R. A., & Thousand, J. S. (2000). *Restoring for caring and effective edu-cation: Piecing the puzzle together.* Baltimore: Paul Brookes.

Waters, J. T., Marzano, R. J., & McNulty, B. (2004). Leadership that sparks learning. *Educational Leadership, 61*(7), 48–51.

Wilmore, E. L. (2002). *Principal leadership: Applying the new Educational Leadership Constituent Council (ELCC) standards.* Thousand Oaks, CA: Corwin.

Wink, J. (2000). *Critical pedagogy: Notes from the real world* (2nd ed.). New York: Addison Wesley Longman.

Wolfendale, S. (2000). *Special needs in the early years: Snapshots of prac-tice.* London: Routledge.

Young, I. M. (2000). *Inclusion and democracy.* Oxford, UK: Oxford University Press.

Zittleman, K., & Sadker, D. (n.d.). *Teacher education textbooks: The unfin-ished gender revolution.* Retrieved March 15, 2005, from http://www.sadker.org/textbooks.htm

Zubay, B., & Soltis, J. (2005). *Creating the ethical school: A book of case studies.* New York: Teachers College Press.

Zukav, G. (2000). *Soul stories.* New York: Simon & Schuster.

Index

**CORWIN
PRESS**

The Corwin Press logo—a raven striding across an open book—represents the union of courage and learning. Corwin Press is committed to improving education for all learners by publishing books and other professional development resources for those serving the field of PreK–12 education. By providing practical, hands-on materials, Corwin Press continues to carry out the promise of its motto: **"Helping Educators Do Their Work Better."**